T0274241

MARCEL PROUST

My Reading

MICHAEL WOOD

MARCEL PROUST

OXFORD
UNIVERSITY PRESS

OXFORD
UNIVERSITY PRESS

Great Clarendon Street, Oxford, OX2 6DP,
United Kingdom

Oxford University Press is a department of the University of Oxford.
It furthers the University's objective of excellence in research, scholarship,
and education by publishing worldwide. Oxford is a registered trade mark of
Oxford University Press in the UK and in certain other countries

Published in the United States of America by Oxford University Press
198 Madison Avenue, New York, NY 10016, United States of America

British Library Cataloguing in Publication Data

Data available

Library of Congress Control Number: 2022951436

ISBN 978–0–19–284582–5

DOI: 10.1093/oso/9780192845825.001.0001

Printed and bound by
CPI Group (UK) Ltd, Croydon, CR0 4YY

Series Introduction

This series is built on a simple presupposition: that it helps to have a book recommended and discussed by someone who cares for it. Books are not purely self-sufficient: they need people and they need to get to what is personal within them.

The people we have been seeking as contributors to *My Reading* are readers who are also writers: novelists and poets; literary critics, outside as well as inside universities, but also thinkers from other disciplines—philosophy, psychology, science, theology, and sociology—besides the literary; and, not least of all, intense readers whose first profession is not writing itself but, for example, medicine, or law, or a non-verbal form of art. Of all of them, we have asked: what books or authors feel as though they are deeply *yours*, influencing or challenging your life and work, most deserving of rescue and attention, or demanding of feeling and use?

What is it like to love this book? What is it like to have a thought or idea or doubt or memory, not cold and in abstract but live in the very act of reading? What is it like to feel, long after, that this writer is a vital part of your life? We ask our authors to respond to such bold questions by writing not conventionally but personally—whatever 'personal' might mean, whatever form or style it might take, for them as individuals. This does not mean overt confession at the expense of a chosen book or author; but nor should our writers be afraid of making autobiographical connections. What was wanted was whatever made for their own hardest thinking in careful relation to quoted sources and specifics. The work was to go on in the taut and resonant space between these readers and their chosen books. And the interest within that area begins precisely when it is no longer clear how much is coming from the text and how much is coming from its readers—where that distinction is no longer easily tenable because neither is sacrificed to the other. That would show what reading meant at its most serious and how it might have relation to an individual life.

Out of what we hope will be an ongoing variety of books and readers, *My Reading* offers personal models of what it is like to care about particular authors, to recreate through specific examples imaginative versions of what those authors and works represent, and to show their effect upon a reader's own thinking and development.

Anne Cheng
Philip Davis
Jacqueline Norton
Marina Warner
Michael Wood

Preface

John Forrester writes evocatively of the figure he calls 'the internal historian of science'. This person 'becomes the past scientist, repeats the processes of struggle, failure and eventual apparent success' [1]. Forrester goes on to quote a passage from Michel Foucault to which I shall return. I am not a historian or a scientist, and I don't have any hope of becoming Marcel Proust, but I was much taken by the challenges to memory and imagination, by the interrogation of the act of reading, that a literary analogue of Forrester's description would imply, and I began to think about a certain question, not unrelated to more familiar ones but different in tone and impulse. The question is: what would the world be like without this work? Where would we be if it hadn't happened? This is how I found myself writing about Proust's work as an event and about events in relation to that work itself.

The largest and most obvious meaning of the word 'event' in this context would be: the life and work of Marcel Proust (1871–1922); the writing that led up to and turned into *A la recherche du temps perdu*; the publication of that work and earlier ones; the later appearance of manuscript drafts and unpublished stories; the recreation of this opus (or pieces of it) in the minds of readers, early and late. My work concerns this event but so do all other books on Proust, and I should try to be a little more specific about what I have in mind.

For some readers, the event really would be all of the above. This was what Bernard de Fallois meant when he said 'Proust's unpublished work doesn't exist' [2]. Provocative words since he was introducing a whole volume of such material and, two years earlier, had brought out *Jean Santeuil*, an unfinished novel that Proust worked on between 1895 and 1899. There is a lot of truth in de Fallois's challenging remark. The year 'when everything changed' [3] had a long history, and Benjamin Taylor is right to suggest that even some of the most casual moments of Proust's early social life turned out to be part of an 'essential preparation' for his later writing [4]. And yet, allowing for different premises and framings, we could invert de Fallois's proposition entirely. The event that finally created the figure we know as Proust did not take a whole lifetime; it occupied certain months, perhaps certain weeks, of a certain year, 1908.

I hope this book as a whole will say something about the event as a lifetime affair, and I shall try to show in my first chapter what the sudden change of 1908 looks like. Other chapters explore events that Proust created or defined or commented on, significant moments of reading and/or writing that would not exist without him. To give simple names to rather complex occurrences, we shall see: a change of track, a distant cause, a national crisis, an incomplete occurrence, a suspension of life, a displacement of justice, a parade of appearances. There could be many more moments of this kind. The chapters move broadly between worlds—between neurosis and politics, let's say—and between romance and the law. But the worlds meet up quite often, and both are full of metaphors and mythologies. A central chapter seeks to explore this profusion in its own right.

Proust himself offers helpful ostensive definitions of the word 'event'. He even borrows the English word. An obituary for his character Charles Swann says that the style and reputation of the deceased 'could not fail to arouse the curiosity of the public in every *great event* of music and painting' [5]. Often Proust finds that the word needs an adjective to point us in the right direction, and then he writes of events that are daily, dramatic, important, indifferent, theatrical, historic, useless, great, slender, minimal. Sometimes, the implication tilts the other way as if events choose their own rank among happenings. 'These visits were an event'; 'it would require an event, it would require a war'. And, at times, the word 'event' carries a whole array of ironies or complications with it, as with the person who 'is no longer a woman but a series of events' (GW 460; SG 477; P 92).

Philologists are wary of the word 'event', as if perturbed by its proneness to exaggeration. 'Something that happens or takes place', the *Oxford English Dictionary* says, 'an incident, an occurrence'. Well, yes, but an event is different enough from other incidents and occurrences for us to want to call it an event. This is often a matter of public relations or just boasting, and the dictionary does include 'something significant or noteworthy' among its definitions. Proust offers an ironic version of this sense when he has his narrator explain that what was an event for him (his arrival in what seemed an impenetrable zone of high society) was nothing of the kind for the Duchesse de Guermantes: 'things which had constituted events for me had passed unnoticed by her' (FT 319).

This is exactly where the interest of the word lies. Who gets to say an occurrence is an event, and why and when do we believe them or not? The dictionary's reference to particle physics brings us closer to the action. An event is 'a highly energetic collision between subatomic particles that produces particles of types not involved in the collision'. Now we're talking: energy, collision, and new types of particles.

Inside and outside of physics, such an event is what marks the arrival of a new paradigm or what Michel Foucault calls an episteme. He doesn't use the word 'event', but his description in *Les mots et les choses* (1966) meets all the criteria for the term. It begins with an act of reading and laughing.

> This book first arose out of a passage in Borges, out of the laughter that shattered, as I read the passage, all the familiar landmarks of my thought—*our* thought, the thought that bears the stamp of our age and our geography ... In the wonderment of this taxonomy, the thing we approach in one great leap, the thing that, by means of the fable, is demonstrated as the exotic charm of another system of thought, is the limitation of our own, the stark impossibility of thinking *that* [6].

The text in question is a paragraph regarding 'a certain Chinese encyclopedia' in which animals are classified in the following way:

> (a) those that belong to the Emperor, (b) embalmed ones, (c) those that are trained, (d) suckling pigs, (e) mermaids, (f) fabulous ones, (g) stray dogs, (h) those that are included in this classification, (i) those that tremble as if they were mad, (j) innumerable ones, (k) those drawn with a very fine camel's hair brush, (l) others, (m) those that have just broken a flower vase, (n) those that resemble flies from a distance [7].

Foucault goes on to say that Borges's mischief doesn't so much wreck the idea of taxonomy or its content as take away the space where either of them could exist.

Borges adds no figure to the atlas of the impossible ... He does away
with the *site*, the mute ground upon which it is possible for entities
to be juxtaposed ...

From there, Foucault moves on to his own preoccupation, the
event that resembles his event of reading. This is the creation of
an 'archeology' that will somehow circumvent the impossibility
of conventional intellectual history.

> Quite obviously, such an analysis does not belong to the history
> of ideas or of science: it is rather an inquiry whose aim is to redis-
> cover on what basis knowledge and theory became possible ... I
> am restoring to our silent and apparently immobile soil its rifts, its
> instability, its flaws; and it is the same ground that is once more
> stirring underneath our feet [8].

I knew without counting that Proust uses the word 'event' a lot in *A
la recherche* and that he loved its mixed implications of certainty and
slippage. But it was only when I started writing (and counting) that
I recognized how much Proustian work the word is doing, how
provocatively it becomes a sort of interpretative magic wand. Here
is a further example of Proust's intriguing usage: 'Events modify
themselves, either because failure amplifies them for us or because
satisfaction reduces them.' Events for Proust are not just what happens, they are also what happens to them. The narrator of *A la
recherche du temps perdu* has been talking of a strange form of satisfaction that I think most of us will recognize: the weird pleasure
of seeing how bad things can get. Then he says:

> There are moments in life when a kind of beauty is born of the mul-
> tiplicity of the trials that assail us, interwoven like Wagnerian leit-
> motifs, as well as of the simultaneous realization that events do not
> fit into the pattern of reflections pictured in the poor little mirror

that intelligence carries before it and calls the future, that they are outside us and appear as abruptly as someone who has come to observe a crime in the act.

(F 411)

The context of Franz Kafka's unsent letter to his father is quite different, but the tone is remarkably similar. When Kafka says that all his bad experiences come 'magnificently' (*großartig*) together, his adverb is the perfect companion (the letter was written in 1919) to the music of Proust's multiplying trials [9].

I have not distinguished dogmatically, or all the time, between Marcel Proust and the narrators of the fiction and essays. There are many voices here, and some are no doubt Proust's own. But there is an important sense in which Proust the person is not Proust the writer: the first of these figures is not made entirely of words, and we can know the second in ways we cannot know the first. Proust himself gives us a choice between what happens when we write and when we socialize:

> In fact, it is the secretion of one's innermost life, written in solitude and for oneself alone, that what one gives to the public [...] What one bestows on [...] conversation [...] or in those drawing-room essays [...] is the product of a quite superficial self, not of the innermost self which one can only recover by putting aside the world and the self that frequents the world.
>
> (BW 79)

A similar choice is on offer (from the narrator) in the following late passage from *Le temps retrouvé*:

> I was thinking about my book in more modest terms, and it would even be a mistake to say that I was thinking of those who would be my readers. For they would not be [...] my readers, so much

as readers of their own selves, my book being merely one of those magnifying glasses of the sort the optician at Combray used to offer his customers […] I would not ask them to praise me or denigrate me, only to tell me if it was right, if the words they were reading in themselves were really the ones I had written.

(FT 343)

I am not writing *A la recherche du temps perdu* as I read it. But I am reading myself as I read Proust, and I am reading, as closely and imaginatively as I can, the words he wrote. For this reason, I have taken most of my cues from Proust's actual language, and this book is, in a sense, a lexical enterprise. Every term we scrutinize leads us into a waiting labyrinth, and some of them, like Ariadne's thread, even help us to find our way out.

Contents

1. Impossible Music   1

2. That Evening   20

3. Dreyfus Time   37

4. The Scenery of the Event   55

5. Profound Albertine   71

6. Proust's Law School   88

7. After the Ball   106

Further Reading   120
Notes   122
Index   129

When Virgil is mentioned, we are not to understand the person of a famous poet called by that name, but only certain sheets of paper, bound up in leather, containing in print the works of the said poet.

Jonathan Swift

1

Impossible Music

I

The 1908 event in Proust's life is dramatic and complex: it includes most of the features that, as we saw in the preface, may inhabit the term. There is a collision between types of writing that produces a type not included in the collision; there is a disturbance of familiar thought and a contemplation of various impossibilities. The ground moves beneath Proust's feet, and uncertainty hovers round the event in the shape of chance, the friend and enemy that Proust can't stop talking about, the agency that keeps reminding us that all of this might not have happened.

Antoine Compagnon suggests that hoping to 'find the key to this miraculous passage' is a 'crazy dream' and perhaps the very idea of a key shows a misunderstanding of what was going on in Proust's mind and life. But since Bernard de Fallois's publication of *Contre Sainte-Beuve* in 1954, most of the texts have been before our eyes, and the stylistic event is not a mystery, at least in hindsight. What is interesting is the choice of descriptions on offer. Compagnon says that Proust is 'juxtaposing philosophy and novel, memory and criticism, without uniting them' [1]. This is true, but I also want to say that something vanishes here: the site on which Proust could write the novel he thought he was writing. He registers this disappearance and decides to write criticism instead.

At this point, at least three things happen. First, writing criticism reveals to Proust that what he had been working on was not *his* novel—or *was just* a novel in a conventional sense. Five years later, about to publish *Du côté de chez Swann*, he recognizes and then contextualizes his departure from the old novel—it is still the form his work departs from least ('c'est encore du roman que cela s'écarte le moins') [2]. Second, his writing about what he can't do, his lyrical farewell to his old project, is so wonderful that it can't be a second-best option of any kind and indeed hints at a literary plot: failure is a great topic. And third, Proust begins to elaborate in this writing a sense of significant impossibility, which hovers in his work from this time on.

I may need to say something here about the varieties of modernist fiction. There is the flagrantly modernist kind, the one that openly abandons old modes. Writers like Woolf, Joyce, Kafka, and Musil are intensely preoccupied with their version of the non-site of classification, the home of confusion. By comparison, Proust and Thomas Mann look rather like nineteenth-century relics, late, stubborn avatars of Balzac or Stifter. Mann himself thought as much for quite a long time—until he read Harry Levin's 1939 book on Joyce, when he began to see similarities where he had only seen dramatic difference. He realized that he also was a modernist, far too ironic to be anything else and more devoted than anyone to what T. S. Eliot called 'the mythic method', the recourse to old stories as 'a way of controlling, of ordering, of giving a shape and a significance to the immense panorama of futility and anarchy which is contemporary history' [3]. Mann, perhaps, would not have spoken of controlling.

Proust's situation is not quite the same as Mann's, although there are many resemblances. Both were writing what Mann called time-novels, and in his foreword to *The Magic Mountain*, Mann evokes 'the extraordinary pastness' of the story he is about to tell.

> It takes place ... long ago, in the old days of the world before the Great War, with whose beginnings so many things began whose beginnings, it seems, have not yet ceased. It took place before the war, then, though not long before [4].

Long ago, not long ago, beginnings that do not end. This looks, at first glance, like a muddled attempt to think about change, but we quickly realize it is something else: a subtle parody of such a muddle and a picture of how we do think of such things—all the time.

In the first pages of *A la recherche*, we read:

> A sleeping man holds in a circle around him the sequence of the hours, the order of years and worlds. He consults them instinctively as he wakes and reads in them in a second the point on earth he occupies, the time that has elapsed up to his waking; but their ranks can be mixed up, broken.
>
> (WS 9)

The narrator goes on to say that sometimes his mind 'would let go of the map of the place where I had fallen asleep' and that, on waking, 'since I did not know where I was, I did not even understand in the first moment who I was'. There is no parody here that I can see, but there is Proust's recurring equivalent, a sort of rhetorical extravagance, a sense of having discreetly left the literal world. In a way, each of the chapters of this book tracks this extravagance, which, I am suggesting, is a major element in Proust's modernism. Compagnon, revising the sense of mere juxtaposition he had seen in the drafts, suggests that 'Proust is our book of books because he reads like Balzac and Blanchot at the same time' [5].

II

The story of the manuscripts of 1908 is perhaps more interesting than the story in the manuscripts, at least as far as the drafts of the abandoned novel are concerned. Among the sources for the material Bernard de Fallois put together under the title *Contre Sainte-Beuve* were what he called 'seventy-five large-format pages, containing six episodes that will all be taken up again in the *Recherche*' [6]. De Fallois printed excerpts from two of them. The rest of the book, a creatively eclectic affair, consists both of subtle essays on literature and criticism and garrulous sketches for articles of social gossip. There are chapters on Sainte-Beuve's critical method, on Nerval, Baudelaire, and Balzac. There are short chapters on sleep, rooms, days, a person called the countess, and what it was like to see your own article appear in *Le Figaro*. The collection also registers Proust's declaration of war on the intelligence and offers a brief elaboration of the memory theory that will come to resolve the supposed riddle of *A la recherche du temps perdu*: where are writers to turn when they have lost all faith in their talent and all interest in reality? [7].

Some time after 1954, when de Fallois's book was published, the seventy-five large pages disappeared, although all of the manuscript material was later notionally deposited in the National

Library. Biographers and critics routinely mourned their loss, and, as Nathalie Mauriac Dyer, the skillful editor of the finally published documents, says, 'the vain inquiries conducted by several generations of scholars since the beginning of the 1960s [. . .] imprinted on the "seventy-five pages" a special mystery and aura' (*Feuillets* 199). What had happened?

In January 2018, de Fallois died, and many of his papers went to the Library. There is still some question, apparently, about the range and the status of the surviving Proust manuscripts. The known papers contained, among many other things, some stories Proust had chosen not to print—edited by Luc Fraisse and published in a volume called *The Mysterious Correspondant* (2019)—and . . . the seventy-five pages. Had de Fallois forgotten he had them? Were they lost among his own papers? Both Fraisse and Mauriac Dyer pick up an interesting archaic French phrase in this context: 'par-devers lui'. It means 'to himself' but is a little more formal than that and etymologically suggests a turning inwards rather than outwards. Fraisse uses it of Proust's treatment of the pieces he didn't want to publish. Mauriac Dyer uses it of de Fallois: 'A Proustian with taste, Bernard de Fallois (1926–2018), had not kept to himself for more than a half-century the least remarkable of the manuscripts of the author of *Swann*' (*Feuillets* 199). The two scholars are almost certainly remembering an exchange in the memoir of Proust's housekeeper, Céleste Albaret, where he asks her if she is burning his notebooks as requested. He suspects her, she says, of keeping them to herself or for herself, 'par-devers moi' [8].

There are apparently seventy-six large pages with writing on them, but Mauriac Dyer and Gallimard kept the magical number seventy-five for their title. The editor calls the six episodes 'An evening in the country', 'The Villebon way and the Meséglise way',

'A stay at the seaside', 'Young Girls', 'Noble names', and 'Venice'. According to her thoughtful chronology, Proust could have begun work on this material late in 1907, but most of it would have been written in the course of 1908. By November of that year, he had temporarily abandoned (or was abandoning) it in order to turn to his book on Sainte-Beuve. Jean-Yves Tadié asks an astute question about this material and this move. 'What was there in these seventy-five pages that was so good that he would write them, so bad that he would stop working on them?' (*Feuillets* 12). We could amplify the query by wondering also how there could be so much of the thematic material of *A la recherche* already in these pages and so little of the style and mood of the novel. There is the beginning of an answer in the rest of *Contre Sainte-Beuve*.

III

The language of Proust's early description of what is left for the failed writer of novels to do is a symptom, a mimesis of logical disarray. 'I have reached the moment', Proust writes, 'when [...] one may be prevented from saying [...] the things one most wanted to say.' That is a brutal parsing of the main clause. Here is an English version of the actual sentence:

> I have reached the moment, or, if you prefer it, I find myself in circumstances where one may fear that the things one most wanted to say—or at least if not they themselves, should a flagging sensibility, which bankrupts talent, no longer allow it, then in their stead those that stood next, which by comparison with this higher and holier ideal, one had come to think little of but which after all one has not read anywhere, which one may suppose may never be said unless one says them oneself, and which obviously stem just as much from

one's mind, though from an even shallower region of it—one may
suddenly be prevented from saying.

(BW 72)

Giving up all hope of doing anything about his 'higher and holier
ideal', Proust turns to what he takes to be the most practical alternative: a critical work centred on Sainte-Beuve, although it would
be 'much more in respect of Sainte-Beuve than about him'. Of
course, Proust may not manage this option either (and didn't),
but the odds look a little better for now. He continues, 'I might
manage to say some things [. . .] about what criticism should do
and what art is.' He would also hope to talk about 'certain forms
of life', and finally, 'leaving Sainte-Beuve quite out of it, I would try
to say what art might have been to me if [. . .]'.

At a later moment, the distinction is not between one kind
of writing and another but between working and not working:
'Never having been able to work I was no good as a writer' (BW
193). This inability is what Proust elsewhere repeatedly calls his
laziness. Still, as we read the materials selected by de Fallois, we
do notice a lessened awkwardness in the writing, and by the time
we come to the last words of *Contre Sainte-Beuve*, we know we are
stylistically (and critically) in quite a different place:

The fine things we shall write if we have talent enough, are within
us, dimly, like the remembrance of a tune which charms us though
we cannot recall its outline, nor hum it, nor even sketch its metrical
form, say if there pauses in it, or runs of rapid notes. Those who are
haunted by this confused remembrance of truths they have never
known are the men who are gifted; but if they never go beyond saying that they can hear a ravishing tune, they will convey nothing
to others, they are without talent. Talent is like a kind of memory
which in the end enables them to call back this confused music, to

hear it distinctly, to write it down, to reproduce it, to sing it. There comes a time in life when talent, like memory, fails, and the muscle in the mind which brings inward memories before one like memories of the outer world, loses its power. Sometimes, from lack of exercise or because of a too ready self-approval, this time of life extends over a whole life-time; and no one, not you yourself even, will ever know the tune that beset you with its intangible, delightful rhythm.

(BW 201)

There are amazing formulations here. We are to be haunted by truths we have never known, and we are to make these truths available to others in writing. If the truths remain elusive, we have nothing. If they become clear, they are probably the wrong truths. 'Talent is like a kind of memory.' Above all, it is a form of labour, of the work that Proust had earlier said he couldn't do. And the notion of time in its most obvious, least reparable sense, allows him the tender, ironic thought that some of us will have been ancient all our lives, even when were young. Too bad. The music was there and we weren't listening.

Will Proust escape this fate? We know the answer, and probably he does too, at this point. Or soon will. This perfect picture of a missed meeting is also the promise of a new start, a commitment to impossible music.

IV

'Every day I set less store on intelligence' (BW 17). This is how *Contre Sainte-Beuve* begins. The statement seems to reflect Proust's ideas about time and quantity closely enough, but it's a little too peremptory to do much else. The intelligence here is the

Sainte-Beuve of our mental apparatus or what Sainte-Beuve might be if he represented French clarity and social good sense at their best. At the end of his preface, Proust insists on the 'inferiority of the intelligence' but also reminds us that this assessment itself belongs to the intelligence. 'It is intelligence we must call on to establish this inferiority' (BW 21).

Both Townsend Warner and Sturrock translate 'intelligence' as 'intellect'. There are good grounds for this move since it signals something of the difference in meaning between the French and English words 'intelligence', identical in their spelling. But there is also a restriction in such a choice since the intellect, in French and in English, is a more limited affair than the intelligence. It is also, especially in English, more easily seen in a negative light, while no one, to adapt Descartes, wants a lower IQ than they already have. The practice of intelligence testing, incidentally, began in France with Alfred Binet, whose *Etude expérimentale de l'intelligence* appeared in 1903 and who introduced the Binet–Simon intelligence test the following year. Proust was not attacking an easily attackable feature of the mind; he was attacking the mind at what almost everyone thought was its reflective and practical best, and I think we need to stay with 'intelligence' to allow this polemic its full range. A rather casual remark in *Contre Sainte-Beuve*, almost a joke, is very helpful here. If we are speaking about a book, Proust says, 'it is almost as stupid to say, "It is very intelligent" as "He was very fond of his mother"' (BW 198). There is quite a lot going on here, but the major point involves the statement of the obvious. Of course, books are intelligent, at least the good ones are—it's the least one can ask. The real question is what else they are, what other reaches of the mind they reflect or represent.

9

For Proust, the intelligence is related to consciousness, the will, naming, understanding, and much of what it used to be fashionable to associate with the concept of reason. Proust's next paragraph after the one about stupidity offers a lucid if slightly romanticized distinction:

> Books are the work of solitude and the children of silence. The children of silence should have no portion with the children of the word—thoughts that owe their being to a wish to say something, to a disapproval, or an opinion; that is, to vague idea.
>
> (BW 201)

There is a wonderful give-away in Proust's first quotation from Sainte-Beuve. Proust reports that it was said of the famous critic that he had 'carried the methods of natural history into the history of moral philosophy' (BW 73). In the process, he made an important distinction between the Ancients and Moderns of traditional critical debates. The snag with the Ancients is that we can't know them personally and can't examine them as if they were a living species. We are, Sainte-Beuve said, 'reduced to commenting on the works' (BW 74). Reduced? I imagine whole armies of New Critics shrieking with indignation, and many readers of other schools and temperaments may think that Sainte-Beuve has made an impeccable case against himself.

Sainte-Beuve continues:

> I do not think of literature as a thing apart, detachable from the rest of the man and his nature [. . .] So long as one has not asked an author a certain number of questions and received answers to them, though these were only whispered in confidence, one cannot be certain of having a complete grasp of him, even though these questions might seem at the furthest remove from the nature of his writings. What were his religious views? How did he react to the

sight of nature? How did he conduct himself in regard to women, in regard to money? Was he rich, was he poor? What governed his actions, what was his daily way of life? What was his vice or his weakness?

(BW 75)

Sainte-Beuve's error, Proust argues, was not so much in the application of his method as in the method itself, which rests on a category mistake. Books are not written by the social self evoked above—or at least great books, or the books we care about, are not. This, Proust says with delicate irony, is 'what a very slight degree of self-acquaintance teaches us': 'that a book is the product of different *self* from the self we manifest in our habits, in our social life, in our vices' (BW 76).

This idea does not belong to Proust alone. We find an earlier version of it in Yeats, who said that the poet 'is never the bundle of accident and incoherence that sits down to breakfast' [9]; and Henry James wrote 'The Private Life', a wonderful short story based on a similar provocation. A version of the argument underlies Roland Barthes's metaphor of the death of the author. Proust's emphasis is different, though. In Sainte-Beuve's method, as in the social chatter Proust loves to write about, the false author is all too alive, and indeed unavoidable. Proust insists on how wrong all this is. Sainte-Beuve could not see 'the gulf that separates the writer from the man of the world', could not understand that 'the writer's true self is manifested in his books alone' (BW 81). Sainte-Beuve was not entirely consistent in this failure, though, since he did write the following sentence, which Proust himself would not have disowned: 'La Bruyère lives entirely in his book; it is there, and nowhere else, that one must seek him' [10].

Proust's theory of the author is closely related to his practice as a critic, which is what a large piece of *Contre Sainte-Beuve* shows in some detail. These pages, we are to imagine, would have been at the heart of the critical work Proust thought he might write once he had given up on the great novel that was escaping him. There is some remarkable close reading. Of Baudelaire's gift, for example, for slowing down one line in order to launch an assertion in the next, which Proust compares to the soaring movement of a trapeze; and, conversely, of the sudden endings of many of Baudelaire's poems, their suggestion of broken wings and failed flight (BW 104–105). Above all, there is the *tour de force* of the essay on Balzac, so rich that I can sketch here only some of its qualities.

It takes the form of a (rather one-sided) conversation with the critic's mother, who died in 1905. 'You're frowning', Proust says, having just mentioned Balzac. 'You don't care for him, I know' (BW 118). And for four pages after this, and at various later moments in the essay, Proust describes, with a sort of kindly patience, all the reasons why his mother is right not to like Balzac, especially his vulgarity. He does treat his characters 'with the naivete of a child who, have given names to its dolls, thinks they really come alive'. He offers us a 'half-baked realism, too fabulous for life, too prosaic for literature' (BW 124). Balzac's writing is pretty loose too. 'He is in such a hurry to state the facts that the sentence is left to shift for itself' (BW 128). But all this is, for Proust, inseparable from what is great about Balzac. 'But you see, the strength of some of his pictures may be due to that same vulgarity.' 'Balzac's style, properly speaking, does not exist [. . .] In Balzac [. . .] all the elements of a style which is still to come exist together, undigested, untransformed' (BW 120, 127). We submit to a writer like Tolstoy, Proust says, regarding him as greater and stronger than we are:

> With Balzac, we know all his vulgarities and at first were repelled by them; then we began to love him, then we smiled at all those sillinesses which are so typical of him; we love him, with a little dash of irony mixed in our affection; we know his aberrations, his shabby little tricks, and because they are so like him we love them.
>
> (BW 133)

The tone here may seem a little condescending, too flavoured by the writer's desire to incorporate his mother's view, but the final effect is just the reverse. Proust wants us to identify with the writer—with the writer as writer, the person found in the words of the poem or the novel—and when we do that, as Ludwig Wittgenstein remarked in another context, there are a lot of things we shall not say.

Proust is identifying, in his way, and inviting us to avoid what later came to be known as the intentional fallacy, the belief that the motive and reasons of the social and historical person known as the author were either available or relevant for literary criticism. Or is he? Surely, considering literary works 'from the point of view of those who wrote them' is precisely the intentional fallacy writ large? It is, until we connect the remark to Proust's comments on the different, secret self of the writer and on listening to the music 'beneath the words' of any text. My sense is that Proust is actually saying that real writers are in large part the reader's invention (although the reverse is also true) and that is why we should and do embrace their defects: not because they are virtues after all but because they are an essential aspect of who and what a writer is.

V

In 1908, Proust's writing about impossibility is most closely associated with the work of Nerval. Mauriac Dyer says that, at one point, 'Proust has become Nerval' (*Feuillets* 231), and I'd like to connect this thought to three textual occasions in *Contre Sainte-Beuve*. First, Proust says that when we read Nerval, 'our pleasure is full of perplexity'. The French word is 'trouble', which he also uses for his memory experiences. Second, he associates Nerval's work with the evocation of what cannot be said: 'When all is said, it is only the inexpressible, the thing one believes one cannot succeed in getting into a book, that remains in it [. . .] But it is not in the words, it is not said, it is all among the words.' Or beneath the words, as Proust says elsewhere in this work. And third he cites a famous line from Nerval's poem 'Fantaisie' in order to show how un-French and untraditional Nerval is, in spite of his reputation for being the romantic representative of Old France. 'What we have here is one of those rainbow-painted pictures, never to be seen in real life, or even called up by words, but sometimes brought before us in a dream or called up by music' (BW 113, 17, 114–115, 110–111).

We could take the provocation of this poem further, building on the intriguing mixture of trouble, the insufficiency of words, and the return of the musical simile. The poem's first stanza runs as follows:

> Il est un air pour qui je donnerais
> Tout Rossini, tout Mozart et tout Weber,
> Un air très vieux, languissant et funèbre,
> Qui pour moi seul a des charmes secrets.

There is a tune for which I would give up
All of Rossini, Mozart and Weber,
A very old, weary, funereal tune,
Which has secret charms for me alone [11].

Proust, I think, finds in the writing of certain pages of *Contre Sainte-Beuve* the kind of tune for which he would give up all reason and philosophy, all sensible discourse. If he had to. With the happy memory experiences recounted in *Contre Sainte-Beuve* and in *A la recherche du temps perdu*, he doesn't have to. He hears the tune and figures out in detail the constitution of its immense attraction. This is what the fairy tale of the last door opening at the end of a long fruitless search is all about. We read it in this form in *A la recherche*:

> But sometimes it is just when everything seems to be lost that we experience a presentiment that may save us; one has knocked on all the doors which lead nowhere, and then, unwittingly, one pushes against the only one through which one may enter and for which one would have searched in vain for a hundred years, and it opens.
>
> (FT 174)

In *Contre Sainte-Beuve*, Proust speaks of the 'resurrection' of certain 'hours in our life' and says it depends, 'like all resurrections, on mere chance'. This is how he sets up the encounter with the pre-madeleine piece of toast, and he repeats the point in the narrative itself: 'My old cook offered to make me a cup of tea, a thing I never drink.' Never except this time. Of course, the tea alone wouldn't do the trick, and Proust mentions chance again. 'As chance would have it she brought me some slices of dry toast.' At first, the writer doesn't understand what the piece of toast is trying to tell him, what he is to make of his sudden sense of 'disquiet, the smell of geraniums and orange-blossom trees, a sensation of extraordinary radiance and happiness' (BW 17). Then he realizes. The 'shaken partitions' of his memory have given way, and he is back among the summer mornings of his childhood, when he would share tea and *biscottes* with his grandfather. We are clearly supposed to think of how close he came to missing the moment, how completely unresurrected it might have been.

And there is another kind of moment that cannot be resurrected, a tune that will not give up its secret. For this challenge, Proust does have to give up reason and much else in order to remain faithful to the beauty and torment of the experience. This fidelity is important because success means nothing if we don't know what sort of failure was waiting in the wings and even more so because Proust wants paradoxically—or not so paradoxically, perhaps—both to promote the fairy tale (miracles do happen) and to register the odds against any such solution.

Having described other resurrected memories that will reappear in *A la recherche*, the text of *Contre Sainte-Beuve* turns to a moving evocation of the failure of one such moment: the sensation is there but without meaning or revelation, however hard the writer seeks to find them. I should say at once that this story, in its later iteration in *A la recherche*, has long been for me one of the greatest passages in the novel, an instance of incomparable richness. It's not that I'm in love with failure, although I do, perhaps, believe that stories of failure often tell us more than stories of success—happy families are, after all, a bit alike. It's that the longing rendered here actually includes the success it can't have because the reality of what isn't happening is so intense.

In *Contre Sainte-Beuve*, Proust says his friends have often seen him pause in front of a group of trees. He asks them to leave him alone for a moment. But he can't recover the memory the trees are pointing to:

> I could not tell where I had seen them. I could recognize their shapes and their grouping, their outline seemed to have been traced from some beloved drawing that trembled in my heart. But I could tell no more of them, and they themselves seemed by their artless passionate attitude to say how sorry they felt not to be able to make themselves clear, not to be able to tell me the secret that they well knew I could not unriddle. Ghosts of a dear past, so dear that my heart beat to bursting, they held powerless arms out to me, like the ghosts that Aeneas met in the underworld.
>
> (BW 20)

He wonders some more about their place of origin. Was it a walk when he was a child, was it one of those imaginary realms where he dreamed his mother was ill ('a dream country only but almost as real as the country of my childhood which was already no more than a dream')? He doesn't know.

A la recherche is even more eloquent about this impeccable, terminal failure. The trees seem to say, 'What you do not learn from us today you will never know', and the narrator confirms this prophecy. 'I never did find out what it was these particular trees had attempted to convey to me, or where I had once seen them [. . .] I was as sad as though I had just lost a friend or felt something die in myself, as though I had broken a promise to a dead man or failed to recognize a god' (SYG 299).

Les Soixante-quinze feuillets contain the answer to the literal question that lingers in this passage (and on into *A la recherche*), 'the key', as Mauriac Dyer says, 'to the reminiscence of the three trees of Hudimesnil' (*Feuillets* 231):

> Often since then, looking at similar trees in Normandy, in Burgundy, I would suddenly feel invaded by a sort of sweetness, and my present consciousness would slip away to allow room for a very old one. 'I have seen these trees, but where?' It was all so vague I thought it was only a dream. And then I remembered, it was the avenue we took when we left the town to take the road towards Villebon.
>
> (*Feuillets* 61–62)

Villebon is the name that will later be changed to Guermantes. But then the mystery opens up again; the key is a delusion because the real message of the trees seems to be the unavailability of their meaning. Continuing to look for a message is a mistake or a disability. Mauriac Dyer writes of 'an anti-intellectualist credo' (*Feuillets* 231). The narrator knows where he first saw the trees, but that is all he knows. The magical experience loses all contact with the past and becomes another instance of reality's failure to live up to any sort of attractive dream, 'the way we imagine each place that we do not yet know, and that we never find when we go there':

> That obsessive desire to exhaust the particularity of a region, and to find words for it has ended up as a sort intellectual discomfort that returned to me in dreams, like physical discomforts.
>
> (*Feuillets* 62)

Rewriting these thoughts a page or so later, Proust says:

> Even today when all the places in the world have one after the other refused access to the mysterious essence I dreamed of for each of them [...] it seems to me that this avenue must really contain something analogous to what I have so often dreamed.

And then he settles for a hypothetical ban as a form of consolation:

> For there truly are things that must not be shown to us. And when I see that I have spent my whole life trying to see these things, I think that is perhaps the hidden secret of Life.
>
> (Feuillets 63)

Each place, never, must not, hidden secret. Proust's later work rarely grants such perfection to hopelessness. Indeed, as we have seen, much of it is dedicated to the fairy tale of the magical moment, the terrible proximity to defeat that finally allows for victory. But we are looking at the large lesson he learned in 1908 and 1909. Learned as a writer, we might say, rather than a thinker—or before he learned it as a thinker. The later version of the story of the trees is theoretically more desolate than the first one. The narrator doesn't even know where he has seen the trees before. And altogether less desolate because to know a mere temporal fact, to know only a temporal fact, is a false victory, is to be stranded in the world of overconfident intelligence. This is not where the example of Nerval leaves Proust. He is learning to live beneath the words or between the words. That is where the unreal pictures find their reality.

2

That Evening

I

I don't believe Proust wanted us to linger too long over the opening sentence of A la recherche. But he surely wanted us to feel a
slight shock at the apparent error, the placing of a past perfect
tense ('je me suis couché') where an imperfect would be correct and expected. And he does write, in an early essay, about
his distaste for the grammatical imperfect, 'this cruel tense that
represents life to us as something both ephemeral and passive'
and that remains, for him, 'an inexhaustible source of mysterious
sorrows' [1]. In translation, Scott Moncrieff's 'used to go to bed'
effectively removes the error. Lydia Davis follows the French literally ('went to bed') but, of course, in English, 'went' could just
as easily be an imperfect tense. A literal English version of what
Proust wrote might be something like 'For a long time I went
to bed early once.' The effect would resemble that of the opening sentence of Dickens's *Little Dorrit*, where a manifest imperfect
tense announces a single past perfect moment: 'Thirty years ago,
Marseilles lay burning in the sun, one day' [2].

It is easy to understand the logic of Proust's move: there are
plenty of recurring events that continue to feel as if they were hap-

pening for the first time. The interest of the phrase is in its stealth, particularly in relation to the word 'longtemps'—we wonder if we know what a long time is—and in its willingness to quarrel with grammar. This is the beginning of many discreet subversions of language in this novel and an announcement of a story about a particular evening, which, for a long time (Proust uses the word 'longtemps' again in this instance), reduced the narrator's memories of his childhood to a single evening of victory and regret, 'as though Combray had consisted only of two floors connected by a slender staircase and as though it had always been seven o'clock in the evening' (WS 46). There is a wonderful representation of just this vision in Stéphane Heuet's rendering of A la recherche as a graphic novel [3].

Hyperbole is a matter of exaggeration, but we can exaggerate downwards as well as upwards. We have just seen Proust reduce a whole village to a fraction of a house and a period of life to a single hour. Hyperbole is everywhere in his writing, and likely to take off in any direction, producing intricate miniature mythologies as it goes. It becomes an instrument of analysis when other instruments seem to fail, where ordinary logical parsing leaves us helpless.

The story we have just seen announced is an excellent case. We read it in Proust's unfinished novel, Jean Santeuil; in a draft for what was not yet A la recherche; in A la recherche itself, recounted early and remembered late (twice). This is not only a surprising myth but also a deep mythologizing of the very idea of story. It shares with many other narratives the post hoc invention of a beginning or of a single beginning where there were probably too many to count. A comparison with the work of another writer may allow us to see all this more clearly; not a large step, in spite of the difference in tone and drift.

In the seventh episode of Joyce's *Ulysses*, set in a newspaper office, various conversations take place, mainly about uses and abuses of language, heroic and unheroic exploits of the word. At one point, a man called J. J. O'Molloy starts to talk about a famous piece of legal rhetoric, pauses, takes out his cigarette case, and offers it to his friends. Someone, probably Stephen Dedalus, but possibly the elusive narrator of the novel, notes the moment and thinks, 'False lull. Something quite ordinary.' And then, apparently tempted by the idea of the quite ordinary into a version of its perfect opposite, adds:

> I have often thought since on looking back over that strange time that it was that small act, trivial in itself, that striking of that match, that determined the whole aftercourse of both our lives [4].

Dedalus and Molloy do presumably have aftercourses to their lives, although we shall never know anything of them beyond this day, 16 June 1904. But there is very little reason to think that they share their aftercourses and no reason at all to think that the striking of the match plays any significant role in their lives. The sentence is a parody of the kind of narrative claim mentioned above: this is when it all began. Don Gifford and Robert Seidman want to associate the parody with 'the Dickens of *David Copperfield* and *Great Expectations*'. As when David, for example, muses on the wedding of Peggoty and Barkis: 'I have often thought since on looking back what an odd, innocent, out-of-the-way kind of wedding it must have been' [5]. This is a good connection, and Joyce plainly is spoofing this kind of memory talk. But my interest lies not so much in the tone as in the rest of the sentence: 'that small act, trivial in itself, that striking of that match, that deter-mined the whole aftercourse of both our lives'. We recognize the genre of the claim, and we recognize, in Joyce's parody, that, in this particular instance, it is entirely false. It isn't funny if it isn't false.

As far as I know, almost no one thinks Proust's narrative claim is false (or funny). I don't wish to suggest that it is false—only that it is enormously strategic and that a writer would have to be very lucky to get a mere bit of family life to do so much work for him on its own. The claim concerns the staggering consequences of a goodnight kiss first withheld from a child by his mother, then demanded by the child and granted by the mother in the context of an intense drama. Here's the claim, made very late in *A la Recherche*, only a few pages away from the end of the whole novel, and some 3,000 pages away (in the most recent French edition) from the initial account of the event itself:

> It was that evening [. . .] that marked the beginning [. . .] of the decline of my will and of my health. Everything had been decided at the moment when [. . .]
>
> (FT 354)

We may also want to think of another version of the claim, quietly offered earlier in the last volume, in which the narrator calls this same moment 'perhaps the loveliest and saddest night of my life' (FT 195). And it may help if we convert the claim into something closer to Joyce's idiom:

> I have often thought since, looking back over that strange time, that it was that small act, apparently trivial in itself, that withholding and giving of a kiss, that determined the whole aftercourse of both our lives.

II

We can track the language of Proust's story in its three versions. The development among them seems slight at first, but the slightness quickly turns into something else. There is no open parody effect, in spite of Proust's exceptional mastery of that mode. Here, the effect feels as if it ought to be that of parody but isn't. It is pathos working too hard, a highly operatic scenario. There is no way back from here to any mundane world of just going to bed. But then we wonder if the pathos is not so much overstated—what would be the measure of moderation?—as insistently extravagant in the manner I have already mentioned, a stylistic gesture hinting at a form of knowledge or a scepticism that will not speak its name. In practice, the different versions work towards a sort of taming or retuning of the opera, defining an achieved effect as the just degree of excess, and we may find it interesting that it is the second instance that seems the furthest fetched rather than the first.

In *Jean Santeuil*, the young protagonist has gone to bed (but not to sleep) and the mother explains the situation to a doctor friend who has come to dinner. The mother is too predictable as a parent here, offering views and idioms that the child might well want to attribute to her, a wish that his friend, the third-person narrator, lavishly grants. She says she and her husband don't want the boy to continue with 'these girlish habits'. They want him to 'grow up to be a manly little fellow'—the French speaks literally of 'a virile education'. She has already half-apologized for the boy by saying he is 'so impressionable'. The doctor smiles and says, 'he is what we should call a nervous subject' (JS 25). The doctor plainly believes that nervous subjects don't exist—they are just people who are not trying hard enough to be like the rest of us. The mother, back on her serious track, says the boy is only seven but she and her husband are already imagining a career for him in diplomacy or the law. Above all, they don't want him to be 'an artist of genius'. We may wonder where that idea came from. They are sitting in the garden and when the grandfather complains of the boy's weakness (he has just called to his mother from his bedroom window), the mother, unconsciously preparing her own downfall, borrows the doctor's term: 'he's so nervous: it's not altogether his fault' (JS 26).

At this point, the narrator treats us to a barrage of epithets for how the boy feels. The moment is 'truly tragic', its 'vague horror' is 'cruel'. And in a quite wonderful use of an ordinary idiom, we learn that, for Jean, it is a matter of leaving the whole world for the whole night, although, of course, 'tout le monde' is the standard French phrase for 'everybody'. There is more talk of 'abandonment', of 'horrible suffering', and the metaphor of the viaticum appears, accompanied by a learned gloss ('the sweet offering of cakes that the Greeks tied to the neck of the dead spouse or friend as they laid them in the tomb, so that they might complete without terror the underground journey, cross the dark realms without hunger' (JS 26).

The boy thinks his mother is 'harsh indeed' to make him suffer so. The narrator says Jean is 'still too young' to understand his parents' educational principle, but actually he seems perfectly to have grasped the whole situation: they want to make him manly, and they are doing everything possible to achieve the reverse effect. The mother has 'blamed his weakness as a fault, as something he ought to be ashamed of', and—here's a beautiful complex sentence—he 'felt obscurely responsible for his agitation, his sadness and his tears which he nevertheless did not have the strength to master' (JS 29).

The mother finally goes upstairs, kisses Jean, comforts him. But then, when she makes a movement to leave, he leaps out of bed, clutches her, and bursts into tears. He rolls around, completely out of control, devoting, we are told in an almost unparsable proposition, 'to the consummation of his fault the violence that remorse wielded against him'. When a servant looks in and wonders what the problem is, the mother says, 'But you can see, Augustin, Monsieur Jean doesn't know what's the matter with him, what he wants. He is suffering from his nerves' (JS 30, 31).

Jean goes to sleep, and the mother returns to the garden, apologizing to the doctor for 'this little show'. He says, 'Fortunately, unhappiness at his age is not a very serious matter', and the narrator intrusively comments on the doctor's perspective: 'It is, perhaps, permissible to hold that Jean was less wrong than the ironical doctor [...] in taking his misery seriously' (JS 31). Jean was not right; just less wrong. The permissible seems a long way from any kind of dogma or virile education. This version of the story ends with an extraordinary sequence of thought. We are told that the words that Mme Santeuil

> allowed herself to say had brought such happiness to Jean, because they had laid to the account of nerves, thereby absolving him from all responsibility, the sobs and screams which had caused him such feelings of remorse, which exercised so deep an influence upon his life. That new sense of irresponsibility which his mother then had publicly recognized in the presence of Augustin—as a nation recognizes a new government—had acted as a guarantee of his personal existence and assured his future. The cruel, the prolific struggles which, from earliest childhood, Jean had been ceaselessly waging against himself, ceased altogether from the day

when the nervous tension against which he had been trying to fight was recognized as something that, though unfortunate, was no longer criminal, so that instead of thinking he must avoid a fault he realized he had only to take care of an illness.

(JS 33)

Pleasure and doom, freedom from guilt, condemnation to illness: there is an extraordinary pathology here and a great illustration of what a word like 'nerves' can do. It's hard not to feel, though, that some sort of sense of triumph prevails, a kind of glee that is not explained by the ostensible analysis. Is it that the boy's life has become a novel instead of the piece of frightened prose it was before? What do we make of the political metaphor of government? Is this anarchy as liberation?

The next draft belongs to 1908 and is written in the first person. It gives us the full operatic chorus from the boy himself, distanced only slightly by time—the time, as it happens, for his mother to die. We don't know his age at the time of the event. We learn that he used to have 'a frightful moment' every night when he had to part from his mother and repeatedly felt that life was 'abandoning' him. There was 'frightful anguish' and what the boy calls 'my torture'. 'Anguish' returns as he says he feels like a condemned man—condemned to die, I think we are to assume. Later, this is a matter of 'atrocious anxiety', and again, 'anguish'. Now the boy is ready to compare going upstairs at home to mounting the steps to the guillotine. His bedroom becomes a prison and 'a labyrinth of pain'. He may have some sense of the extravagance of all this since he speaks of 'the theatre of my torture'. But then he may be thinking only of a stage and not of a style. The idea of incarceration is doubled; his bed is 'the prison in the prison' (*Feuillets* 31–36).

27

At this point, we get an excursion in time that does not appear in any other version and that we have been able to read only recently, with the publication of the seventy-six pages of manuscript that were believed to be lost. The excursion is quite sudden and begins in the middle of a long sentence. The boy waits, the mother appears, she is wearing a white dressing gown, 'her admirable black hair' is let down. And then a subordinate clause effectively introduces the story of a whole life. The main clause of this complicated proposition is 'Her hair [. . .] framed a face':

> Her hair, in which there was all the sweetness and all the power of her nature, and which survived for such a long time as the unconscious vegetable growth of the ruins she is tenderly protecting from the ruin of her happiness and of her beauty, framed at that time a face of adorable purity, gleaming with intelligence, with a lively sweetness that sorrow could never extinguish, but that kept ahead of life with a hope, an innocent gaiety that very quickly disappeared and that I never saw again except on her death bed when all the sorrows life had brought her were erased by the hand of the angel of death, when her face for the first time in so many years no longer expressing sorrow and anxiety, returned to its original form.
>
> (Feuillets 40–41)

The story continues with later memories of the mother, especially the ones perceived 'on the obscure roads of sleep and dream'. The narrator writes of 'the days that broke her life [. . .] prepared her death'. Her face is tired and red, her eyes tired. She is walking fast, almost running towards a railway station. On her face there is 'a sort of irritation that was the form of her suffering passing through her health'. The son doesn't think he is to blame for all this but acknowledges his part: 'She was accusing me a little.' The excursion ends with 'I started to run after her' (Feuillets 41).

Or these could be the first words of the return to the goodnight narrative since the boy does now ambush his mother as she comes upstairs. She says, 'if you don't go to bed immediately I will never speak to you again'. Then she relents and the boy sees, 'for the first time in my life', that she might perhaps regard tears as a sign of sadness or disorder rather than just misbehaviour. This sounds like an improvement but the boy wants to arraign his mother as well as embrace her. The text offers a wonderful phrase here: 'She had just consecrated as an illness that which she had tried to cure by never recognizing it as an illness [. . .] this concession was a first disappointment, a first abdication.' She, 'so brave, so determined to overcome the obstacles of life', was now 'confessing her impotence'. 'It seemed to me that I had hurt her', the narrator says with considerable understatement, 'or rather had made her smaller [. . .] that I had managed to pervert her will and her reason, that that was my victory' (*Feuillets* 43). What in *Jean Santeuil* was a change of government for mother and child becomes the mother's abandonment of all rule. The boy feels sorry for her but not as sorry as he feels for himself. And not as sorry as he feels guilty.

In *Du côté de chez Swann*, there is no initial change of a regime, no new plan for the boy. The mother just doesn't come and say goodnight when there are visitors. There aren't many, but Charles Swann is a regular caller at the child's uncle's house in the country. A sort of twinning between Swann and the narrator begins here. The next part of the volume ('Un amour de Swann') is a long flashback into Swann's earlier life, and Swann will never know how far his emotional career has foreshadowed the narrator's sentimental education.

On this occasion, the grandfather says the boy looks tired and should go to bed. The father agrees, and this means he won't even get a kiss downstairs. He has to leave without his viaticum but offers no gloss in this version. Now the images pile up. His bed is a tomb, his nightshirt a shroud, he is going to bury himself in his sheets; again, we meet the figure of the condemned man. 'Anguish' makes its appearance too, although this time accompanied by an interesting theory about its relation to love. I'll come back to this because the theory has many branches.

The boy sends a note to his mother via a servant, and she replies that there is no reply. Then the boy has a brilliant, desperate idea. He won't go to bed, he won't try to sleep, he will wait up for his mother and waylay her as she comes upstairs. This is the most terrible thing he has ever done, and he assumes they will send him off to boarding school tomorrow, but so what.

The mother arrives but the father is following her, and the boy thinks this is the end—'I'm done for'. The father, unpredictable as many autocrats are, doesn't think there is any problem in the mother staying with the child—in fact, she could stay the whole night if she liked. He is wrecking, in a moment, a whole disciplinary plan, but he doesn't see that. Right now, he is feeling kind, and inadvertently slips into the boy's repertoire of metaphors: 'we are not executioners'. He also makes a joke that recalls the tone of the doctor in *Jean Santeuil*: 'I'm not as high-strung as the two of you' (WS 39).

The mother does stay the whole night and the boy again sees this as what we might call the moment of original exemption, an unheard-of crime not only not punished but also rewarded by an unheard-of benefit:

And so, for the first time, my sadness was regarded no longer as a punishable offence but as an involuntary ailment that had just been officially recognized, a nervous condition for which I was not responsible; I had the relief of no longer having to mingle qualms of conscience with the bitterness of my tears, I could cry without sin.

(WS 41)

As in the 1908 draft, the change of government becomes an abdication. The mother no longer certifies the new regime; there is no new regime, only the failure of the old. The release from guilt abruptly turns into its opposite: guilt on all sides. The mother abandons her post, and the child, knowing what this costs her, fails to help her stay there:

I ought to have been happy: I was not. It seemed to me that my mother had just made me a first concession which must be painful for her, that this was a first abdication on her part before the ideal she had conceived for me, and that for the first time she, who was so courageous, was confessing herself defeated. It seemed to me that, if I had just gained a victory, it was over her [...] it seemed to me I had just traced in her soul the first wrinkle and caused the first white hair to appear.

(WS 41)

Proust's narrator attributes this perception to the child, not the later writer, and it makes a curious, intuitive sense for him to do so. The child imagines that his mother is ageless until his own behaviour starts the clock. She becomes old not through the action of time but because of his faults. So much for the new government and her abdication. Nothing has changed in their relationship, even though he is claiming everything has. He always knew she would leave him one day and that she would be immortal unless he misbehaved. As, of course, he would misbehave.

III

This is the dossier in the case of the goodnight kiss. One night represents the moment when a person on the borderline between health and illness became ill for good and, conversely, gave up the strenuous struggles with his own weakness which constitute the moral life—or, if you like, the moral life of the French bourgeoisie circa 1880.

This is a wonderful example of the work of narrative, of memory being invaded—even colonized—by narrative, and I am not really concerned with the putative confession about Proust's own history that seems to be lurking here. Still, it is instructive to see what the biographers think. André Maurois, George Painter, and Ghislain de Diesbach have no doubts. We are reading, in Maurois's words, 'the narrative of a scene that certainly occurred in Marcel's childhood' [6]. Painter is so sure of this that he quotes from *Jean Santeuil* with an altered name: 'Master Marcel doesn't know himself what is the matter with him' [7]. Roger Duchêne, the only real sceptic I have managed to find, devotes a whole chapter to what he calls, after Truffaut, 'Stolen Kisses'. 'We are taken in', he says. 'One would swear that little Marcel really did live through this exceptional evening' [8]. Jean-Yves Tadié makes clear that 'no letter, no external document' exists outside the fiction to confirm the story. Still, taking exactly the opposite tack from Duchêne, he invites us to think of the frequency of fact rather than the flourish of romance. 'The crucial scene of the novel emerged from an event that, far from being unique, as in the work of art, was often repeated with the sad banality of life' [9]. My own sense is that the believers are likely to be right about the history but that the writing is so confected that we need to think seriously about the confection. That is why I am invoking the example of Joyce and the idea of mythology.

Such moments are mythological not because they don't happen, or can't happen, but because they are overloaded and can't signal the definitive change they promise. They are often flatly contradicted by the aftercourse (if there is an aftercourse) of the lives they are supposed to have altered. Neither Jean Santeuil, nor Marcel Proust, nor the narrator of *A la Recherche* ceases to feel responsible for his nervous condition or settles into the life of the morally carefree invalid. The interesting question is why a story that can't be true is so important for its teller.

This, I have long thought, is one useful definition of myth: a story that feels like a fiction but is driven by needs that are far from imaginary. Commenting in his diary on his early plays, *Baal* and *The Jungle of the Cities*, Bertolt Brecht wrote, 'We are on the scent of a mythology here' [10]. We get a kind of double inhalation; the scent of something not quite right and the scent of urgency in the story. The story has to be told because it's not quite right.

Proust's story apparently concerns a lost paradise of health and willpower, the moment when those 'forces' were intact. But, of course, they never were intact; that was the whole point of the parents' regime. They were trying to give him the health and the willpower they thought he didn't have, and then one day, in the story, they gave up trying. He didn't lose a paradise he had, only the paradise he now feels his parents should have provided for him: a sort of inheritance they failed to deliver. But—and here is the lurking strength of the myth—the narrator is about to embark on a huge narrative project, one that will require all the health and willpower he hasn't got. What is more, if the narrator of this novel even faintly resembles the writer of the novel we have just read, he is quite a long way into this same project, already having demonstrated and put to use enough health and willpower for several lifetimes. The last door of the fairy tale opens because you're lucky but also because you have stubbornly knocked on a lot of doors. There is more than a paradox or a contradiction here. It's not just that Proust's narrator must richly possess the willpower he claims to lack. It's that he possesses it because he can claim to lack it, he can't have it unless he believes he lacks it, the myth is essential, the supposed disability is deeply enabling. Proust's narrator needs to tell himself this story so that he can write his book, that is, tell another story. And, in this sense, the myth is true: the fatidic evening doesn't alter everything, but the story of the fatidic evening does.

There is an interesting separate development of the narrative claim. In *Du côté de chez Swann*, the narrator inserts a later reflection into the story of the goodnight kiss; that is, he looks back from the same distance as on the last pages of the book. Of course, the whole narrative, as distinct from what is narrated, belongs to this later time, but this passage makes the time lag clear, indeed is about the time lag and about how time has passed and not passed. The reflection appears just after the father has suggested the mother spend the night with the boy and just before the mother offers her 'official' recognition that the child's problem is 'regarded no longer as a punishable offence but as an involuntary ailment':

> This was many years ago. The staircase wall on which I saw the rising glimmer of his candle has long since ceased to exist. In me, too, many things have been destroyed that I thought were bound to last forever [. . .] It was a very long time ago, too, that my father

ceased to be able to say to Mama: 'Go with the boy'. The possibility of such hours will never be reborn for me. But for a little while now, I have begun to hear again very clearly, if I take care to listen, the sobs I was strong enough to contain in front of my father and that did not burst out until I found myself alone again with Mama. They have never really stopped; and it is only because life is quieting down around me more and more now that I can hear them again, like those convent bells covered so well by the clamour of the town during the day that one would think they had ceased altogether but which begin sounding again in the silence of the evening.

(WS 39–40)

This part of the story could clearly be translated into the Joycean idiom as marking a moment that determines the aftercourse of a life. But there are differences too. There is no explanation here, no apportioning of blame, no diagnosis either in the past or the present. There are only the sobs; the sobs are all that is left. The house is gone, the parents are gone, much of the inner life of the narrator has been destroyed, but the sobs have never stopped. This claim is hyperbolic and metaphorical but not, I think, mythological in the sense that the other claims are. It seems to me that in these sentences we are seeing something like the persistence of memory, the loyalty of the mind to what once was. In the other cases, the narrative is doing almost all the work, and it scarcely matters whether there is a memory at all. The difference allows us to think of the past in contrasting ways: as what we make of it and as what it makes of us. As the story that we tell, let's say, and as the ongoing story that we are.

This is an important, self-evident meaning of the word 'memory': not forgetting. But we need its other meaning too: the rescue of what was forgotten. How could we remember it otherwise? Walter Benjamin characteristically puts these double activities together, tilting his case towards the second. 'The important thing for the remembering author', he says, 'is not what he experienced, but the weaving of his memory, the Penelope work of recollection. Or should one call it, rather, a Penelope work of forgetting?' [11]. What Benjamin is suggesting, I think, is that we can rewrite the sobs, and we do. But we can't forget them, or, rather, we can forget them only in the special sense of forgetting Proust creates for us: surrounding ourselves with noise.

3

Dreyfus Time

I

The Dreyfus Affair poses many questions, more than we can count, perhaps. One of them runs regularly through Proust's work, even when he is not thinking of justice, or the state, or anti-Semitism. It is the question of knowledge: how we attain it; what we do when we don't have it; and, more disturbingly, what we do when we don't want it. The Affair, as seen by Proust, or as we see it through Proust's eyes, becomes an extraordinary textbook for the study of these concerns.

We are looking at the model of an event as Alain Badiou describes it: neither neutral nor natural [1]. We may also think it looks like history's version of Borges' encyclopaedia, a pile of parts that know no whole. Joachim Kalka suggests that 'ultimately it is impossible to briefly summarize what happened in the Dreyfus Affair', not only 'because of the intrigues, forgeries, and cover-ups that accompanied the investigations and legal proceedings from the start' but also because of the 'background of dizzying political vicissitudes, constant government shake-ups, coalitions, resignations, the toppling of ministers' [2]. Ruth Harris writes of 'a cocktail of contradictory fears and beliefs' and 'a seemingly incoherent world of feeling' [3]. Genuinely incoherent, perhaps, but we can pick our moments and preoccupations.

When, in 1898, Emile Zola published an open letter to the President of France in the newspaper *L'Aurore*, recently founded by Georges Clemenceau, who himself added the title 'J'accuse', the whole basis of the argument was the innocence of the wrongly condemned Alfred Dreyfus, who was accused of passing on secret French military information to the Germans. Yet, the word that appears most frequently in the letter is not 'innocence' but 'crime'. Zola does not mean treason, Dreyfus's supposed offence, but the crime (or crimes) involved in the 'terrible judicial error' of condemning the wrong man. The 'real crime', he says, is 'the dreadful denial of justice' from which France is suffering, as from a disease [4].

The accusation and arrest were not crimes to start with, Zola says, just the results of carelessness, prejudice, and stupidity. But to convict a man on the basis of 'crazy novelistic imaginings' is a 'prodigy of iniquity', and Zola mockingly lists the 'crimes' Dreyfus was presumed to be guilty of, as well as treason:

> he speaks several languages; not one compromising paper was found in his house; he sometimes visits the place where he was born; he works hard, he likes to know things; he doesn't worry; he does worry [5].

Almost everything about the Dreyfus Affair, except the captain's innocence, remains notoriously murky. Proust suggested at one point that it had ceased to look like something out of a novel by Balzac and had become 'so Shakespearean' [6], meaning like a play full of twists and apparent resolutions. And when Zola said that Dreyfus had been invented by a major in the French army, he meant not that the major had created the person but that the unfortunate captain had been conscripted for a long-running serial based on non-facts.

We could take this condition as emblematic of what modern murk looks like. The great Victorian symbol of confusion was the fog of Dickens's London, inherited by Sherlock Holmes and Jack the Ripper, and analysed by Oscar Wilde:

> There may have been fogs for centuries in London. I dare say there were. But no one saw them, and so we know nothing about them. They did not exist until Art had invented them [7].

But this was a moral fog. It was a matter of things going wrong in such a way that no one knew how to set them right. There was no doubt about what was happening. It was the way out that was masked by the fog. More recent confusions, from the conviction of Dreyfus to the assassination of John Kennedy and beyond, are different. We could probably find our way out if we knew what was happening. But that is what we don't know. We don't doubt that there are facts, of course. What we doubt is whether there are enough of them or whether we can detach them from the fictions that hide them and enable them.

Zola was tried and found guilty of libel. The 'real crime' had begun earlier. The formal inquiry into Dreyfus's supposed espionage took place between 14 and 19 December 1894 and essentially uncovered nothing at all. At this point, the wonderfully titled Statistics Section of the French army (the name for the department that took care of military counter-intelligence) started genuinely criminal activities, using documents they knew could have nothing to do with Dreyfus to incriminate him, and re-editing old documents to make them sound more suspicious.

Even during the court martial, it seemed as if Dreyfus might be acquitted. Three key incidents prevented this. One was the decision to hold the proceedings in a closed session. The second was the dramatic request of Commandant Joseph Henry to be recalled as a witness. Back on the stand, he put on a great performance as the loyal old soldier, as French as they come, and swore on his honour, pointing at a picture of Christ that happened to be hanging on the wall, that Dreyfus was guilty. It may be that the trial was effectively over at that point. There was one more thing, though. After the formal proceedings were done, the judges, and no one else, received more supposedly incriminating documents in what came to be known as the secret dossier. This was totally illegal, but, as Jean-Denis Bredin puts it, 'not a single judge appears to have suspected that such a communication, concealed from the defense, was in violation of the law, the Military Code, or common equity' [8]. This failure to suspect is important because, in the world outside, the unanimous verdict of honourable men was a quite proper reason for believing in Dreyfus's guilt. There were plenty of fanatics and anti-Semites who didn't need any kind of reason, of course; but most people would have called for no more than this verdict. Dreyfus was publicly degraded on 5 January 1895 and sent to Devil's Island in February. The case didn't really open again and become internationally famous until 1897. Zola's *J'Accuse*, as we have seen, appeared in 1898.

The second verdict on Dreyfus's guilt was rendered on 9 September 1899, and ten days later he was formally pardoned for what he had not done. A year later, an amnesty was declared that let the conspirators off completely. A mollifying general spoke of closing the doors of forgetfulness on the whole show.

The celebrated Affair was over. Except that it wasn't. The doors were nowhere near closing. As late as September 1905, Dreyfus was hoping that he would soon be able to 'reach the goal of my life' and be 'delivered from this nightmare' [9]. The rehabilitation finally occurred in July 1906. Dreyfus received the *Légion d'honneur* the same month and rejoined the army in October. He retired the following year but re-enlisted in 1917 and fought at Verdun.

II

In Proust's unfinished novel, *Jean Santeuil*, portions of the Dreyfus Affair are seen from close up, but the seeing is scrupulously, almost perversely, non-partisan. I may be wrong about this since, as Géraldi Leroy says, 'the narrator does not hide his Dreyfusard sympathies' [10]. Still, the disclosure may not be incompatible with what I take to be the narrative angle. The boy Jean, some ten to twelve years younger than his author at the time, attends various court sessions associated with the case: the trial for libel of Emile Zola; the testimony of Colonel Picquart, a crucial figure in the uncovering of Dreyfus's innocence; the hearing of expert witnesses on the handwriting of what came to be known as the *bordereau*, the document Dreyfus was said to have given to the Germans. The boy's interest, and that of the third-person narrator, are focused less on questions of right and wrong than on the Affair as a generator of exciting daily news, to be eagerly gathered and passionately discussed.

Two of the ten pieces of the novel identified by its editors as being 'around' the Affair [11] remind us discreetly that this Proust event, as a matter of writing, includes a lively attention to the non-event, the piece of the story that didn't happen. In the second of these passages, Jean doesn't go to the court session because he has to deliver a message to the Opéra Comique, where he meets a director and various singers.

The other instance is a spectacular, ironically overwritten account of the failure of expectation and event to meet up. The audience in the courtroom is very agitated because there has been disagreement about a piece of evidence, and General Boisdeffre has been called to give his opinion on the matter. He is the Chief of Staff of the French army and, in the excited style of the narrator voicing public opinion, a man 'who, had he wished, could have been President of the Republic or even Emperor' (JS 323). The same public, in French collectively called 'one', chatters away:

> Twenty past twelve: it'll take a bit of time to get to the Ministry: he can't be here in less than fifteen minutes. What's he going to say? It's been the general opinion for some time that he wanted to testify. This time the Minister can't refuse permission [. . .] What will he say? The end's in sight now [. . .] If he says one thing, then Dreyfus'll be back in a week from Devil's Island, if another, well then, old chap, it's all over. No one will ever be able to say a word in his favour again!
>
> (JS 324)

Boisdeffre arrives and his appearance is described in detail: tall top hat, stiff leg, hesitance in his walk, eyes blinking as a kind of tic, his hand tugging on his moustache from time to time. His coat looks rather ancient and doesn't fasten properly, but he passes muster as 'a man of very high rank'. The description repeats itself, the suspense continues, everyone is waiting to hear the general's thought, 'still unknown to any but himself, though already formed, which suddenly would burst from the privacy of his consciousness, and change not only the life of one man and one family, but the whole course of European affairs' (JS 326).

Then Proust quietly drops his favourite phrase into the narrative: 'just when' ('au moment où'). 'Just when' the general reaches the small corridor that leads to the Court of Assizes, 'several people' interrupt his progress. Why? Because the president of the court has suspended the session, postponed it until tomorrow. The general is not surprised and leaves quietly. The crowd is 'disappointed and relieved' at not hearing his 'all-powerful words'. The narrator speculates that the president of the court was worried about 'possible diplomatic complications should the Chief of Staff make a statement before the Government had been informed of what was in the wind' (JS 325) but, of course, the real beneficiary of the change of direction is our author, who needed the anti-climax and is astonishingly indifferent to everything except the audience's excitement.

A certain line of thought links most of the other Dreyfus passages in *Jean Santeuil*. At the centre of the argument is what the narrator calls an 'activity' motived by 'an internal and disinterested object'. Such activity is the only meaningful kind for him, and everything else is 'formalism', which we might translate into a contemporary idiom as being busy, fashionable, full of opinions, influential, even important, but entirely at the mercy of what is out there, what people are making a fuss about. A symptom of this behaviour is uncontrolled hyperbole. A small event 'means revolution' or 'the end of the Republic'. The narrator also describes the adepts of formalism as 'fraternizing in the same fever' and as 'assembled crows [. . .] flapping and cawing' (JS 331, 332).

Jean feels Colonel Picquart, the only senior officer in the French intelligence service who has come to believe that Dreyfus is innocent, is to be distinguished from this crew because he is 'a philosopher, man whose whole life, in spite of his sky-blue uniform, had been spent in seeking by the light of reason [. . .] the truth of everything that might, with some urgency, involve a degree of self-examination'. It is true that Jean is 'disappointed but at the same time fascinated' by Picquart's failure to offer any of the signs of having an interior life, of understanding his own situation, and he twice compares the colonel to 'a Jewish engineer' (JS 333, 335), whatever that means. But Picquart is still a hero because he is, again, a 'philosopher'. Such people think not only for themselves but also sometimes at a serious cost to themselves. The narrator mentions Socrates in the *Phaedo,* where his own impeccable logic leads to the necessity of the philosopher's death.

Another passage shows Jean romantically admiring expert witnesses because they are 'men of science who on a point of professional honour had come to the Court to tell the truth, a truth with which they were concerned simply and solely because it was something they had been taught to cherish in the conduct of their art'. For them 'truth was really something which existed in itself and had nothing to do with opinion' (JS 350, 351).

A more complicated notion of truth emerges from what I take to be an invented anecdote, where Proust offers an extraordinary counterfactual theory of the act of espionage at the heart of the Dreyfus Affair. At a social gathering, General T, who was closely involved in the investigation, affirms his view with great precision: 'I can tell you this, that though I do not believe Dreyfus was guilty, I am quite certain that Esterhazy wasn't.' We shall return to Esterhazy, the actual spy, in a little while. Another guest asks who then was the guilty party, and the general says he can't answer. 'It was somebody pretty well-known, and if, in a year or two from now we meet again, I will give you his name.' The conversation continues into the general's complex view of Picquart as both an honest man and a forger, but, meanwhile, the narrator says of history that its 'special and slightly equivocal charm' makes it different from actuality ('it never derives its authority from appearances') and different from the truth too ('it is not a deductive process and hovers between truth and appearance'). As the general talks, the narrator says, 'an immaterial presence seemed to be hovering about the room which might be described as the truth of historic fact' (JS 357, 358).

We may feel there is too much confidence in this view, even allowing for the hovering ghost, and too great an investment in the authority of a single person, as with Picquart himself and the men of science in the earlier sections. But the narrator is speaking for Jean, who is very young, and there is something deeply intriguing about the revelation of a historical truth in a fiction and nowhere else. I think the suggestion here concerns not the conception or availability of the truth but what the truth might have to look like if we are to continue, despite many disappointments, to believe in its existence.

III

The Dreyfus Affair is first evoked in *A la recherche* as a historical moment, a sign of the times, or a sign of time, perhaps, and this essentially is what it remains for the narrator. Society changes its looks 'after the manner of kaleidoscopes', and with the Affair, 'the kaleidoscope shuffled its little tinted shapes':

> All things Jewish were displaced and [. . .] hitherto nondescript nationalists came to the fore. The most brilliant salon in Paris was that of an ultra-Catholic Austrian prince. If instead of the Dreyfus

Affair there had been a war with Germany, the kaleidoscope would have turned in a different direction. The Jews, who would have shown to everyone's astonishment that they were patriotic, could have kept their position; and no one would have wished to go, or even admit to ever having gone, to the Austrian prince's.

(SYG 92)

The narrator's chief point is that people who don't like change are very good at refusing to see it. 'Each time society is briefly stable, those who live in it imagine that further change is ruled out, just as, having seen the advent of the telephone, they now wish to disbelieve in aeroplanes' (SYG 92).

The idea of change can trouble us (or console us) in other ways, and it is striking how often thoughts of the Dreyfus Affair, for Proust and his narrator, creep into what seems to be quite alien territory. 'When we look at faces, they do not appear to be changing' (SYG 468). This is the narrator's reflection on meeting a group of young women at Balbec. But they will change a lot, and we can get a glimpse of this alteration ahead of time. 'To see one of these girls standing beside her mother or her aunt was to glimpse the remoter reaches of ugliness to which [. . .] the features of most of them would have come less than thirty years later.' These as yet absent features are:

as deep-rooted and inescapable as Jewish clannishness or Christian atavism in people who believe they have risen above their race [. . .] as fated as others' Dreyfusism, clericalism, national and feudal heroisms, which the fullness of time suddenly summons from a nature predating the individual himself [. . .] from which he draws his sustenance and in which he dies, without ever being able to distinguish it from the particular motives he mistakes for it [. . .] Our mind [. . .] contains particularities which we think we have chosen. All we can grasp, though, is the secondary ideas, while the first

46

cause (Jewishness, French family, etc.), which gives rise to them, and which we respond to at a time of its choosing, remains beyond our ken.

(SYG 468–469)

These are amazing analogies for a young man's thought about a group of young women, and, rather startlingly, the narrator, prolonging the metaphor of the budding flower with which he began this discussion and which appears in the title of the volume, suddenly gives up the whole idea: 'But, now that it was time for the buds to blossom, what did that matter?' (SYG 469). He was plainly trying to work something out, but what? Is it that one alternative to the refusal to see change would be to see nothing else and so lose the present time altogether? Or are we looking at a deeper anxiety about first causes and how little we know of them?

The Duc de Guermantes becomes the object of a very good piece of comic sociology. He is senior vice-president of the Jockey Club and fully expects to become president when the current incumbent dies. We are told of his 'caring little for this presidency', but this is true only as long as he thinks he is about to get it. Confident of his chances, he doesn't campaign, but others do. Against him. They say his wife was a Dreyfus supporter, that the duke himself was 'half a German'. Losing the election, the duke claims that his 'long-standing friendship with Swann' was the problem, that is, his relationship with someone who was both Jewish and a Dreyfusard. The Dreyfus Affair, the duke says, with spectacular insincerity, had 'caused so much unhappiness'. The narrator reminds us that 'in reality' the duke 'was conscious of only one instance of unhappiness, his own failure to win the presidency of the Jockey Club' (P 31–32).

The duke gets nastier as the conversation continues. Of course, the Rothschilds:

> are Dreyfusards at heart, like all Jews [...] If a Frenchman commits theft or murder, I don't feel I have to say he's innocent, just because he's a Frenchman like me. But the Jews will never admit that one of them could be a traitor, even though they know it's true, and they don't care in the least about the terrible repercussions [...] that can result from their friend's crime.
>
> (P 33–34)

'All the Jews defend a traitor', he says, 'because they're Jews themselves', and he defies his wife to think differently. She does think differently, making one of the rare thoughtful remarks anyone is allowed to make on this topic in *A la recherche*:

> Perhaps it's just because [...] they know that a man can be a Jew without having to be treacherous and anti-French, as M Drumont apparently would have us believe. Certainly if Dreyfus had been a Christian the Jews would not have taken such an interest in his case, but they did, because they realize that if he hadn't been a Jew, people wouldn't have been so ready to believe him a traitor a priori'.
>
> (P 34)

The duke says, 'Women don't understand anything about politics' and announces that 'France should expel all the Jews' (P 34). The satire is broad here. The effect becomes more subtle as we recognize the deeper movement of thought. The duke's behaviour is too buffoonish to be true but also too true to be disbelieved. Just like reality at times.

The Dreyfusards don't receive the same kind of treatment, but they are not exactly supported either, and the narrator's view often seems close to that of Ruth Harris: 'the Dreyfusards [. . .] were often unable to appreciate the philosophical hazards of the deeper tensions in their position' [12]. In *A la recherche*, several of them, including Zola and Picquart, as well as the journalist and politician Georges Clemenceau, the lawyer and historian Joseph Reinach, and Dreyfus's lawyer Fernand Labori, are compared as a group to the Committee of Public Safety, not the most liberal or cherished organ of the French Revolution (SG 149). And when, much later, the narrator draws attention to Reinach's achievements as a defender of Dreyfus and the truth, the tone is very close to an anti-Semitic critique of a Jewish plot:

> In two years he replaced a Billot ministry by a Clemenceau ministry, brought about a complete change in public opinion, got Picquart out of prison to appoint him, for no thanks, to be Minister of War.
>
> (GW 293)

The phrase 'for no thanks' is a gratuitous attack not on Reinach but on Picquart, but the larger question concerns the attribution of all the events to Reinach. He doubtless had a part in some of them, but he didn't arrange any of them single-handedly, so what game is being played by suggesting that he did? We could say the narrator is not as much of a Dreyfusard as his author, but that only displaces the question.

Two later Dreyfus moments in *A la recherche* return to and correct propositions made in *Jean Santeuil*, the first concerning the idea of the privileged witness, the second the conception of scientific truth. In the first, we eavesdrop on a conversation between the narrator's friend Bloch and the diplomat de Norpois. De Norpois answers Bloch's questions by effectively saying nothing, and the narrator explains what is happening. Or rather gives us four possible entertaining reasons for De Norpois being elusive:

> he was 'such a fierce anti-Dreyfusard' that he hated the government as much as the Dreyfusards do, only from the other end;
> what he wants from politics is 'something deeper, situated on another plane';
> his 'political wisdom' applies only to form and procedure and not to real issues;
> it is 'dangerous' to talk about the real stuff.
>
> (GW 237–238)

The narrator then goes on to talk of Bloch's naivete in believing that Norpois could have told him everything. 'For Bloch was in no doubt that M de Norpois knew the truth about all these matters. How could he fail to know it, given that he was a friend of all the ministers?' (GW 238). The fantasy under attack here is not the occasional existence of such truth but the deep belief in its guaranteed presence. The narrator also suggests that even if there are facts and documents in such cases, they are like x-rays awaiting interpretation. In the Dreyfus Affair, even a famous forgery and confession and suicide (those of Joseph Henry) were read differently by different minds.

The revision of the earlier view of science is even more striking and again makes the act of interpretation central. The narrator starts with three interesting locations of inquiry:

> During the Dreyfus Affair, during the war, in medicine, I had seen people believe truth to be a kind of fact, believe that ministers or doctors possess a yes or no to what the patient has without interpretation, believe that men in power knew whether Dreyfus was guilty [...] There is no moment in my life which would not have served to

teach me that only coarse and inaccurate perception places everything in the object when the opposite is true: everything is in the
mind.

(FT 223)

The last phrase burns all the bridges the paragraph has perhaps
unintentionally been building, and we shall learn most from what
Proust's narrator is saying if we see it as too hasty and too simple.
The triplet of truth, fact, and mind is a useful bundle, especially
since 'esprit' also means spirit or wit, and perhaps doesn't place us
so entirely inside our heads as opposed to in the world.

The proposition slips smoothly into a very particular philosophical lineage and also, curiously, both matches a claim and
enacts a misunderstanding. Nietzsche says there are no facts, there
are only interpretations; Derrida seems to say there is nothing
outside the text; and Proust says all facts are attendant upon some
sort of interpretation. Interpretation is the path from fact to truth,
from the materials of the truth to its larger story. This is not the
place to linger and mess up my attempt at clarification, but both
Nietzsche and Derrida, to give them credit, are saying something
more subtle than they have famously been taken to be saying. The
full context of Nietzsche's remark, which became a marvellous
mantra in the days of Deconstruction, is this:

> Against the positivism which halts at phenomena—'There are only
> facts'—I would say: no, facts are just what there aren't, there are
> only interpretations. We cannot determine any fact in itself: per-
> haps it's nonsense to want to do such a thing. 'Everything is subjec-
> tive', you say: but that itself is an *interpretation* [13].

And Derrida was not talking about texts as opposed to something
else, he was borrowing a metaphor from a textual world. He said

'Il n'y a pas de hors-texte' [14]; that is, the book of life doesn't have any unnumbered pages, pages that don't count in the total. We can take this to mean quite a few things, but 'there is nothing outside the text' is not one of them. Proust did not mean to say terminally that everything is in the mind, just that we do live in what Rilke called the interpreted world. Rilke added, it's worth noting, that 'we are not very reliably at home' there [15].

IV

The Dreyfus Affair teaches us, among many other things, that evidence is easily faked and that, when fakes don't work, you can plead national security: you claim to have documents you can't show. There is a real difference between a document that isn't produced and one that doesn't exist. But we have to ask who can see or certify this difference, who controls its display, and what sort of model of probability or prejudice we are going to use in the absence of facts. 'As for those who have made themselves my executioners', Dreyfus wrote in his diary while still on Devil's Island, 'ah, I leave their consciences to them as judges when the light is shed, when the truth is revealed, for sooner or later, everything in life is revealed' [16]. Not quite everything, perhaps.

In Proust, by implication, and in history, by considerable amounts of valuable research and analysis, we seem to be left with two major perspectives on the Dreyfus Affair. They are not contradictory, but they are not the same. The first lingers in the place where this chapter began, in the extended confusion of events which can be described in detail but not brought together into any real coherence. There are too many plotlines; the case feels as if it is made of several different novels randomly mixed and left to themselves. In such a world, the only dependable law is that of chance, which is not a law at all. There is a remarkable instance of the force of this element right at the start of the Affair. It is possible that there would have been no Affair at all if the Minister of War, General Mercier, had been more secure in his political position and if he had not rashly declared to *Le Figaro*, as early as 28 November 1894, three weeks before the trial, that Dreyfus's guilt was 'absolutely certain' [17]. It really did seem, from that point on, that either Dreyfus was going to be guilty and Mercier could stay in his post or that Dreyfus was going to be innocent and Mercier was gone.

The other perspective has an air of prophecy about it. It doesn't concern the Affair's political consequences, good and bad, but rather its standing as a landmark of a (relatively) new interpretative order, a realm where the model of the person most at home with available knowledge is not the scholar or the reporter, or even the spymaster, but the double agent. This is where we are if we pause over the fictions surrounding Ferdinand Walsin Esterhazy, the real criminal. He was a great fabulator, as Marcel Thomas calls him [18], and a crook by any standards. But he managed to persuade many people to act for him, promote him, change his postings, lend him money, and get him out of trouble. He died in England in 1930. In the last version of his story, he says he and not Dreyfus wrote the famous fake document, and he was indeed acting as a German spy. But only acting. He was part of the sting operation the Statistics Section was running, and so the document was a plant, not a surprise.

Is there any evidence to support Esterhazy's story? No. But why would there be? How could there be? In order to believe Esterhazy, we don't have to alter the rest of the story by a jot. We just have to add him to the roster of the Statistics Section. I'm not suggesting that we do this. In fact, I believe, with Thomas and most people, that Esterhazy has brilliantly made the whole thing up. But when we don't know the truth, we need to think hard about why we believe what we believe. We should name the reasons that are enough for us and say what we have when we don't have reasons. In such conditions, we are better able to understand how an unmistakable judicial error could shift from the world of Balzac to the world of Shakespeare without getting any nearer to the truth.

We could say that many aspects of Proust's writing are symptoms of the atmosphere created by the Dreyfus Case. We could also say, more abstrusely but perhaps also more accurately, that the Dreyfus Case itself was a symptom of the time in which Proust was writing, a time when fiction was often escalated into fact, when deceptive appearances frequently took on their own historical reality. As I have suggested, the actual innocence of Alfred Dreyfus does not belong to this scene; it lingers from an older, apparently less manipulated world. But then new epistemes always drag pieces of old ones with them. That's how we know they're new.

4

The Scenery of the Event

I

I have suggested that Proust, like Thomas Mann, often looks as if he belongs to the world of the old novel rather than the new. The Foucauldian shaking of the conceptual ground has not taken place. The prevailing order is in good shape; we just need to be imaginative with our metaphors and invoke a scientific law from time to time. This is partly a historical condition. Proust's education and the state of French philosophy and psychology around 1900 make him the heir of a language and a logic that deal in radical certainties. But then he and his actual language work wonders with this problem, and his examples keep undoing his arguments, as if he was secretly writing his version of Borges's Chinese encyclopaedia.

He begins to build a theory of the need for double-mindedness or many-mindedness. I don't think this theory is ever coherently completed, but it is everywhere in *A la recherche du temps perdu* and very persuasive in spite of (because of) its failure to cohere. Metaphor is an important part of the project, for obvious reasons, but it is an instrument and not, as the narrator of *A la recherche* suggests in a much-quoted passage, an ambitious endpoint.

Proust gives a new meaning (in advance) to the title of an Ian Fleming novel and a well-known movie: *You Only Live Twice.* Twice is better than once, we have to suppose, but Proust's recurring claim is far more radical. He is saying that we don't even have one life until we have the second. This is obviously the case with the famous memory moments where *then* and *now* become a single instant. Time is not regained, it is resurrected, or perhaps even simply awakened—it was never dead, only asleep, like the princess in the fairy tale. There is also the predominance of analogy in Proust's writing. He does write plain, undistracted prose occasionally, and he is very effective when he does. But it can seem as if no sentence of his ever quite stays where it is supposed to be, can't survive without extensive travel to other times and countries. The narrator of *A la recherche* writes of 'the miracle of an analogy that had made me escape from the present' (FT 180), but the escape is often more broadly from any single space or time.

The extravagances may make us think of English metaphysical poetry and the habit attributed to John Donne and decried by Dr Johnson, where 'the most heterogenous ideas are yoked by violence together' [1]. Indeed, Malcolm Bowie does write of Proust as 'a metaphysical wit possessed of a strong liking for physics' [2]. The connections would be a matter of names, images, and contexts rather than ideas, and the elements are not so much yoked together as invited to wonder why they are meeting like this.

Here is a characteristic example, both moving and funny. The narrator of *A la recherche* is about to leave Paris for Balbec and invites us to think about what it means to travel by train. Railway stations, he says, are 'wonderful places' but 'also tragic places'. They are the starting point of a journey we wish to make but they also mark the spot where 'we must abandon all hope of returning to the familiar bedroom which we left only a moment before'. Weather and architecture endorse our feeling since we are faced with a vision of an ominous sky seen through the glass roof of the Gare Saint-Lazare. The discreet allusion to Dante and the specially orchestrated sky—don't trains leave on sunny days?—seem to be the joint product of the narrator's old anxiety about place and his current willingness to mock it a little. But even if we have caught this double tone, and even if we have read the sentence quite a few times before, I don't think we can be ready for the way it ends. We are looking at:

> one of those vast bleak skies, dense with portents of pent-up tragedy, resembling certain skies of Mantegna's and Veronese's, fraught with their quasi-Parisian modernity, an apt backdrop to the most awesome or hideous of acts, such as the Crucifixion or a departure by train.
>
> (SYG 224)

The flipping of the comparison, making the paintings look like Paris rather than Paris look like the paintings, is witty and controlled, and, of course, it's tough to sleep away from home if you're worried about those things. But the Crucifixion? Literally, Proust writes, 'the erection of the Cross', which makes the connection even more managed and intimate. Jesus is not there yet, and neither is the narrator.

In another writer, this performance would be a satire, and a certain critical perspective on indulged hysteria is not absent here. Later in the novel, Proust mentions 'those neurasthenics whose exhaustion is doubled when it is pointed out to them that they are exhausted' (GW 43). But mainly he is doing what he so often does:

exaggerating wildly and also implying that *only* an exaggeration will get us anywhere near the truth of the matter.

Here is another example, interesting in this context because it involves taking a figurative expression literally. Mme Verdurin, the hostess of a significant Paris salon, and a personage who will haunt the novel, ultimately becoming the Princesse de Guermantes, a conversion that is itself a sort of cartoon of what is happening to French society, needs to express her appreciation of her guests' wit but can't laugh. Physically, that is. She can't leave her guests' talent show unregistered either and so resorts to a 'ruse of incessant and fictive hilarity':

> At the mildest remark [. . .] she would utter a little cry, tightly close her bird-like eyes [. . .] and abruptly, as if she had only just had time to avoid some indecent spectacle or avert a fatal blow, plunging her face in her hands [. . .] would appear to be doing her best to suppress, to annihilate a fit of laughter which, had she given way to it, would have caused her to faint.
>
> (WS 208)

This performance repeatedly leaves the lady's husband 'in despair' because he is anxious to be 'as affable as his wife', and the only social weapon he possesses is ordinary laughter. Meanwhile, Mme Verdurin, 'dazed by the gaiety of the faithful, drunk with good-fellowship, scandal and approbation [. . .] poised on her perch, like a bird whose seed-cake has been soaked in warm wine, sobbed with affability' (WS 209). The mildly awkward double appearance of the bird analogy is part of the mood.

What has created this pantomime? Alas, Mme Verdurin dislocated her jaw some time ago, laughing with what she thought was appropriate excess at a joke by one of her guests, and she can't risk doing it again. The concept of sobbing with affability is wonderful, as is the social satire contained in the notion of physical injury through over-acting. But Proust (and/or his narrator) has another touch to add, a matter of language use rather than anything else. Mme Verdurin did not dislocate her jaw through bodily violence—or not only through this. She was also resorting to one of her most characteristic modes of interpretation: 'taking literally the figurative expressions for the emotions she was feeling' (WS 192). This information reaches us in a subordinate clause—the main clause is about laughing at funny stories—that also includes the mention of Mme Verdurin's need to have her jaw reset.

Lydia Davis doesn't try to replicate the joke here. The host and hostess 'shriek with laughter', and the lady has her accident. The noise was presumably not the cause of the damage, and there is no question of literalization except as a general principle. Scott Moncrieff gets a little closer with 'split with laughter'. In French, the verb is 's'esclaffer', which has the sound of English laughter in it and is quite old—Rabelais uses it, for example. And even without knowing anything about the word beyond what is implied by the context, we see how the Proustian gag works. The word describes an action—an application to a French face of what in English would be rib-cracking or a matter of laughing one's head off—that is always taken metaphorically. Except by Mme Verdurin.

II

Proust doesn't use the word 'metaphor' often. Only twelves times in *A la recherche du temps perdu*, for example, by my double-digital count (fingers and computer). Most of the uses are quite casual. When the narrator wishes to illustrate his youthful admiration for the writer Bergotte, he says, 'I wanted to possess an opinion of his, a metaphor of his, for everything in the world' (WS 97). Charles Swann doesn't explain, at a social event, that 'he had merely been speaking metaphorically' (WS 343). 'I can see you have no ear for metaphors', Monsieur de Charlus says to a companion, 'and are indifferent to the history of France' (SG 16). And when the editors of the Pléiade edition of *A la recherche* invite us to look at 'the definition of metaphor according to Proust', they refer us to a passage that doesn't include the word 'metaphor' at all. Proust is objecting to a literary tendency 'which makes the image the purely practical and utilitarian servant of reason'. He thinks this is all wrong. 'No, the image must have its reason for existence in itself, its sudden, entirely divine birth' [3]. An interesting proposition, and one that helps us to understand many aspects of Proust's work. But the editors' casual treatment of image and metaphor as synonyms may seem surprising.

A teacher of English literature (or an English-speaking philosopher) could get a little worried. A metaphor is not just an image, it is a rhetorical assertion of identity. It says that *x* is *y*, not that *x* is like *y*. The teacher's or the philosopher's French counterpart may not see (or may say she does not see) what the problem is. Of course, the metaphor is a comparison, not an assertion of actual identity; everyone knows that. And if this scholar wishes to distinguish metaphor from anything, she will turn not to simile but to metonymy, the image drawn from a local context rather than hauled from some distant conceptual country.

It may help if we complicate this imagined discussion a little. We could start by recognizing the absence of a word for 'simile' in French. There is 'comparaison', but that means exactly what its English counterpart means: a broader and not necessarily

THE SCENERY OF THE EVENT

rhetorical affair. The more interesting question rests not on a choice of words but on the possibility of a delicate difference between the assumptions inhabiting the two languages. It may be that when we think of metaphors in French, we relax our devotion to literal meaning or accept that it is relaxed enough already. In English, we register the literal nonsense in the figure and then see what the nonsense allows us to see.

There is an instructive journey towards such understanding in the novels of George Eliot, a writer Proust loved. In *The Mill on the Floss*, the narrator disapproves (or pretends to disapprove) of metaphor altogether:

> Oh Aristotle! if you had had the advantage of being 'the freshest modern' instead of the greatest ancient, would you not have mingled your praise of metaphorical speech [. . .] with a lamentation that intelligence so rarely shows itself in speech without metaphor—that we can so seldom declare what a thing is, except by saying it is something else [4]?

By the time she is writing *Middlemarch*, Eliot sees metaphor as a kind of destiny: 'for we all of us, grave or light, get our thoughts entangled in metaphors and act fatally on the strength of them' [5]. We can't just 'declare what a thing is' and hope for the best. And at one point in the novel, Eliot devises the perfect metaphor for metaphor. Of a person who has not imagined a certain possibility, she says, 'he did not live in the scenery of such an event' [6].

Even if he is parsimonious with the word, metaphor for Proust (and not only for his narrator) is at one point synonymous with style—'only a metaphor can give a sort of eternity to style', he says in an essay on Flaubert [7]. This is a little too emphatic. Nothing can be guaranteed to grant eternity, and one can write terrible prose full of metaphors. But Proust had been thinking about versions of this proposition for many years before 1920, and his articulations of it allow us to see something of the forest of worries and implications that lies behind the aphorism.

III

In *A la recherche*, the word 'metaphor', when not used casually, assumes strange and interesting meanings. Elstir's paintings are all local, representations of land- and seascapes around Balbec, and the narrator says he 'could see that their charm lay in a kind of metamorphosis of the things depicted, analogous to the poetical device known as metaphor' (SYG 415). Is metaphor analogous to metamorphosis? Proust's narrator may be moving a bit too quickly, but he is certainly suggesting that metaphor can suspend identity, rather than assert it, and that art can be a reverse creation, a decreation, to borrow a term from Simone Weil. 'And if God the Father had created things by naming them, Elstir recreated them by removing their names, or by giving them another name.' Metaphor becomes a mischievous, liberationist art. Names, so helpful to us in so many contexts, may also be the enemies of perception and understanding: 'The names of things always express a view of the intelligence, which is foreign to our genuine impressions of them, and which forces us to eliminate from them whatever does not correspond to that view' (SYG 415).

The narrator goes on to say that, in the mornings and in the evenings, looking out of the window in his Balbec hotel, he would sometimes, thanks to an effect of sunlight, think that a dark part of the sea was a distant coast or look at a blue patch and not know whether it belonged to the sea or the sky. The intelligence corrects this impression. Or more literally, it reintroduces the divisions that mere perception was ignoring: 'The mind quickly redistributed the elements into categories which the impression had abolished.' We are the heart of Proust's idea of the divine birth of the image here. Actively, it creates links, relations. And also, perhaps more importantly and more frequently, it resists separation, categorization. This is exactly what occurs in the example the narrator gives next:

> Similarly, in my room in Paris, I had heard sounds of squabbling, almost rioting in the streets, until I linked them to their cause, for instance the rumbling approach of a dray, the sound of which, once identified, made me eliminate from it the high-pitched discordant shouting which my ear had really heard, but which my mind knew is not made by wheels.
>
> (SYG 415)

The statement is confusing, but deliberately so, because anything that clears up the confusion will clear up too much. The squabbling or the rioting is real as long as its source is supposed but not checked; figurative once the source is established. Error would be one name for metaphor in this case, although metaphors often can't be true or false, just effective or not. But then the chance of error, even in a territory where it is not supposed to be any sort of threat, suggests an interesting counterpart: the chance of truth where there is supposed to be only fiction. The bland way of saying this would be to claim that imagined realities are real in their way, and Proust does claim this again and again. But the criss-crossing chances are more dynamic and place us more firmly in a world of risk. This is what the narrator's apparent *non sequitur* also suggests: 'Those infrequent moments when we perceive nature as it is, poetically, were what Elstir's work was made of' (SYG 415). Seeing nature as it is means not knowing whether you are looking at the sea or the sky, and, as Christopher Prendergast meticulously shows, the narrator's comma is essential: 'as it is, poetically' is not the same as 'as it is poetically'. 'Instead of the relativity of different ways of seeing [. . .] we now have the absolutist claim whereby one way of seeing [. . .] is affirmed as superior to all others in revealing nothing less than the truth of nature' [8]. This is what Elstir teaches us in one of his 'most frequent metaphors', 'the one which compares the land to the sea, blurring all distinction between them'. This is more than a metamorphosis. We probably ought to call it a deconstruction. As in this example:

> It was to a metaphor of this sort—in a painting showing the harbour of Carquethuit, which he had finished only a few days before, and which I looked at for a long time —that Elstir had alerted the mind of the spectator by using only marine terminology to show the little town, and only urban terms for the sea.
>
> (SYG 415)

IV

When, in *Contre Sainte-Beuve*, Proust registers the reasons he can't write novels, he talks about the talents that led him to think he could. First, as we have seen, there is his ear as a reader, his ability to hear an author's tune, the song beneath the words. Second, there is another gift 'for discovering a profound affinity between two ideas or two feelings' (BW 193). He doesn't speak of metaphor in this passage for what I take to be a most interesting reason:

metaphor is only one way of doing what he has in mind, a particular form of a much larger habit or ability. He repeats the thought
of 'these affinities between two ideas' and connects it to an 'inter-
mittently acknowledged self', calling him 'this young man who
thus plays among my ruins'. Proust writes a tiny novel around
this adventure: 'he creates the idea and is created by it, he dies but
an idea revives him'. The young man:

> must be the same as he whose sharp true ear can likewise distin-
> guish a subtle harmony that others are deaf to between two impres-
> sion or two ideas. Who this being is I cannot say.
>
> (BW 193)

He does know this, though:

> He cannot be fed by what there is in a picture by an artist, or a book
> by a writer, nor by a second picture by the artist, a second book by
> the writer. But if in the second picture or the second book he per-
> ceives something which is in neither the first nor the second but
> in some way exists between them, in a sort of ideal picture which
> he sees projecting itself in spiritual substantiality out of the pic-
> ture, he has been given his meat, and begins to live and be happy
> again.
>
> (BW 194)

Proust's invocations of doubleness can seem quite incidental since
they are often buried in longer, different arguments concerning
impressions, for example, or memories: 'Every impression is double, half-sheathed in the object, extended in ourselves by another
half' [9]. The narrator works at 'finding in my memories, for each
being offered by life and forming something like the half of a cir-
cumstance, the being whose adaptation to the former created the

complete event' [10]. But the recurrence has its effect even if we don't pause over it. We get the sense of a person hankering for a double life, as I have suggested, or already living a double life and not sure what to do about it. Or, more precisely, perhaps, someone whose life is only occasionally double and who finds an inexplicable happiness in those moments. For this person, the comic accident I talked about earlier in this chapter, caused by a character's 'taking literally the figurative expressions for the emotions she was feeling', would represent a kind of hell, a condemnation to a single world. I should add that I think this person would find the restriction solely to the figurative just a hellish as a confinement in the literal.

It is intriguing that when the narrator returns to this topic in *Le temps retrouvé*, aggravating his despair as a preparation for the flutter of miracles that will release him from it, he does so by means of a pastiche, one of his old evidences of the boy's existence and talents. He has just read, as a bit of bed-time entertainment during his stay at Gilberte's country house, a long passage from the *Journal* of the Goncourt Brothers or, to be precise, from Proust's brilliant parody of such a passage, an echo of the piece he published in *Le Figaro* in 1908. But now, even his old gift has become a disability, for a moment at least: 'I had never concealed from myself the fact that I did not know how to listen, nor, as soon as I was not alone, how to observe.' As always happens when Proust gets close to abdication, though, he immediately qualifies his view. 'My incapacity [. . .] was yet not total' (FT 23–24). He didn't know how to listen and watch like a person publishing a famous journal or a writer of naturalist novels or a like a piece of audio-visual recording equipment. But there are other ways, and the young man playing among the ruins reappears, considerably older now, of course:

> There was in me a character who knew more or less how to look, but this was an intermittent character [...] The character looked and listened, but only to a certain depth, so that my observation did nor benefit from it [...] What people said escaped me, because what interested me was not what they wanted to say, but the manner in which they said it, in so far as this revealed their character or their absurdities, or, rather, the object that had always been the aim of my researches [...] was the point that was common to one being and another.
>
> (FT 24)

The narrator compares himself to a geometrician, who sees the 'linear substratum' of things, says he himself wants to go 'beyond appearances themselves, in a zone set slightly further back'. This proposition makes him think of another analogy. 'However often I dined out', he says, thinking of the endless social life that animates the Goncourts' *Journal*, 'I did not see the other guests, because when I thought I was looking at them, I was in fact radiographing them.' It's an easy step from here for him to regard himself as mapping 'a cluster of psychological laws', the scientific result of the metaphorical x-ray, but a few more pages of worrying about the matter takes the narrator back into his gloom: 'Goncourt knew how to listen, as he knew how to see: I did not' (FT 24, 25, 27).

The situation is very different when viewed from the other side of the miracle memory moments, which occur later in the same volume. Now, the narrator is ready to launch extraordinary, unrepentant claims for his gifts or for the amazing good fortune that made them active and central to his writing. Metaphor is not essential to this argument, which involves a lot of literal and factual perception of memories whose reality cannot be denied and doesn't need to be played with. But metaphor is still there as an instance of double thinking. The following much-quoted passage not only begins with a metaphor—'an hour is not just an hour, it is a vessel full of perfumes, sounds, plans and atmospheres'—but also contains an implication that metaphor is already somehow implicit in literal language:

> What we call reality is a certain relationship between these sensations and the memories which surround us simultaneously [. . .] a unique relationship which the writer has to rediscover in order to bring its two different terms together permanently in his sentence. One can list indefinitely in a description all the objects that figured in the place described, but the truth will only begin when the writer takes two different objects, establishes their relationship, the analogue in the world of art of the unique relation created in the world of science by the laws of causality, and encloses them within the necessary armature of a beautiful style.
>
> (FT 197)

A certain relationship, a unique relation. There is a lot we have to take on trust here. But it is clear that style includes the tune beneath the words as well as the words themselves—'beautiful' means what it would mean if a mathematician spoke, as mathematicians do, of a 'beautiful' proof—and the narrator has found an answer to the worries that followed on his reading of the Goncourts. And at the end of the sentence, we do meet the word 'metaphor', explicitly linked to the talent for seeing double:

> Indeed, just as in life, it begins at the moment when, by bringing together a quality shared by two sensations, he draws out their

common essence by uniting them with each other, in order to protect them from the contingencies of time, in a metaphor.

(FT 198)

'Just as in life' is a little mysterious, but we need to remember that chance, not the narrator, has created the most interesting pairings of past and present, and it is life itself, he is arguing, that offers the materials for metaphor and sometimes tilts the offering in extraordinary ways. Life is a kind of author here, keen to make its own contribution to whatever fiction is in play. It is also likely to be a better writer than many literal authors; more inventive, less predictable than those who have only 'the poor little mirror' of the intelligence as a scene for their projections. Events 'rarely come singly', the narrator says. 'The sentiments aroused by each of them contradict each other', and this can be very helpful because fear, for example, 'is at least a temporary and fairly potent emetic for emotional troubles' (FT 411). We shall return to this fear and these troubles in Chapter 5.

The idea that the relation between the two parts of a metaphor is analogous to the relation of cause and effect in science does not seem very plausible. But the implied resemblance, perhaps, is not between metaphor and causality but between the roles metaphor and causality play in their respective worlds. I'm tempted to read the narrator as saying that the relation he is talking about, the relation perceived and then caught in words, the meeting of sceneries in style, while not reasonable or predictable or regular is just as firm and central in art as any law is anywhere else. Such a line of thinking will take us straight back to Proust's 'definition' of metaphor. The image is not the servant of reason, and it must have its own (often unreasonable) grounds for existence. In this light, the last phrase of the definition comes into a sense of its own. We understand the abruptness and divinity of the image, the role of the Muses in its creation, the relevance of their own definition of their work as we read it in Hesiod's *Theogony*: 'We know how to tell many falsehoods that seem real: but we also know how to speak truth when we wish to' [11].

5

Profound Albertine

I

'Angoisse' is a key word for Proust, early and late. The usual English equivalent is 'anguish', but in varying contexts it also seems to mean 'anxiety', Angst, and even just fear. We might say that in Proust's many uses of the word it means 'anguish' when it is most visible, acknowledged, and even theatrical; 'anxiety' when it is more secret and pervasive; and Angst and fear at almost any time. When the narrator of *A la recherche* tells us, for example, that the pleasure he 'should have been able to experience' with Albertine 'was in fact perceived only inversely, through the anxiety I felt when she was not there' (FT 184), the translator's word choice seems exactly right. But then both terms work well for the narrator's aphorism that 'after a certain age our loves and our mistresses are daughters of our anguish/our anxiety' (F 471).

A crucial feature of the first love story *A la recherche* tells at length, in the second section of *Du cote de chez Swann*, is its deep reliance on the anguish of uncontrollable uncertainty. As long as Swann knows where his mistress, Odette de Crécy, is, the affair is a routine liaison, a social requirement, almost something of a bore. When, one night, he can't find her, he falls desperately in love, joining the long list of the helpless victims of 'angoisse'.

Love is the occasion to which this anguish 'is in some sense pre-destined, by which it will be hoarded, appropriated'. For the narrator as a boy, this destiny has not arrived, and anguish has to make do without romantic love: 'it drifts as it waits for it, indeterminate and free, without a particular assignment, at the service of one feeling one day, of another the next, sometimes of filial tenderness or affection for a friend' (WS 33–34). And just before the story of Swann in love is about to be told, the narrator picks up his notion of anguish as 'in some sense predestined' to the orbit of love and writes in an intriguing metaphor of 'that anguish which later emigrates into love, and may become for ever inseparable from it' (WS 185). This anguish has no country until it finds one. It has a cause, or causes, and we usually know what they are. But it is also metaphysically stateless or causeless, exists prior to any actual incarnation. In this understanding, it is a sort of magical doom, rather like guilt in the world of Franz Kafka or error in the Catholic doctrine of original sin.

In this way, anguish becomes a model of desire. As we have seen, it is 'born in a particular, anguished moment of our relation to a person, born of our uncertain hold on that person and the fear that he or she may escape' (P 65). It is not always unappeased. But the terms of appeasement are too special to last. We would need not to marry our mother, as Oedipus did, but to remain the child whose longing for his mother's love was not always in vain. Anguish comes and goes—for a while. And then, one day, the anguish emigrates, leaves the family, so to speak, and all it can do is want what it can't have. The narrator actually says it was 'impossible' for him 'to seek peace from Albertine as I had from my mother', adding, 'I no longer knew how to say "I am sad"' (P 99).

II

'Profonde Albertine': the words appear as the verbless main clause of a sentence situated very close to the end of *A la recherche du temps perdu*. Scott Moncrieff translates the phrase literally—'profound Albertine'—and Ian Patterson makes a small move towards interpretation: 'The depths of Albertine' (FT 357). Both versions sustain the mystery of the proposition pretty well, and the context makes clear that the depths are not within Albertine, they are the depths she brings to mind, a sort of semantic and psychological ocean that surrounds her.

The narrator's understanding has changed over the course of the five volumes since he met Albertine in Balbec. He no longer thinks her naïve; he even calls her intelligent. He also believes her to be crafty and elusive, but none of this suggests depths of any kind. The context I have mentioned, a doubly darkened world, is named immediately in the rest of the sentence we are looking at: 'whom I saw sleeping, and who was dead' (FT 357).

The narrator presumably watched Albertine sleeping quite often, especially when she was what he called his captive, but at one point he goes out of his way to describe himself indulging in it. He sounds rather like Dracula contemplating an unconscious victim, although far more tormented by the availability of rare pleasure than the Count was likely to have been. Albertine's sleep, the narrator says, 'realized, to a certain degree, the possibility of love', that is, removed everything that otherwise got in love's way:

> When I was alone, I could think about her, but she was not there, she was not mine. When she was there, I could speak to her, but was too far removed from myself to be able to think. When she was asleep, I did not have to speak any more, I knew she could not see

me, I did not have to live on the surface of myself. By closing her eyes, by losing consciousness, Albertine had put off, one by one, the various marks of humanity which had so disappointed me in her, from the day we first met [. . .] She had drawn back into herself all the parts of her that were on the outside, she had taken refuge, enclosed and summed up in her body. Watching her, holding her in my hands, I felt that I possessed her completely, in a way I never did when she was awake.

(P 60)

The trick is that he can 'dream of her and look at her at the same time' and, in that fashion, experience 'a love for something as pure, as immaterial, as mysterious as if I had been before those inanimate creatures that we call the beauties of nature'. He says, 'I was never so happy as when watching her sleep' and later declares, 'I had set sail on Albertine's sleep' (P 61, 62).

What depths are these? It is clear that this possibility of love excludes all others. Albertine is not dead, but she has, in this lurid account, shed all her human characteristics and is compared to the inanimate beauties of nature. She is also, the narrator claims to think, entirely in his possession, no longer free to deceive or disappoint him (the verb *décevoir* here seems to have both meanings) in any way. There is an element of coprophilia since if she is not a doll she is a corpse, although it is mitigated by the narrator's lyrical concentration on Albertine's breathing, 'a mysterious, murmuring emanation, gentle as a soft breeze over the sea, fairylike as the moonlight' (P 60). To think of sleep is to remember, consciously or not, that it ends in waking.

This memory is the reason why the dreamy portrait of a sleeping figure revives the Albertine the narrator thinks he has got rid of, brings back everything he imagines he is tired of seeing and hearing when she is awake. He stumbles into this perception when he says that 'whole races, atavisms, vices slept in her face' (P 61); but the larger effect is more dramatic and more pathological. His fantasy is to cancel Albertine without killing her, to replace everything she is and means to him by a zombie purity that cannot bother him in any way, by a partner who never disturbs his impossible peace. He would be free of what Christopher Prendergast calls his 'paranoid obsession with the "legibility" of the beloved' [1]. Writing this description, and presumably during the recurring scene that gave rise to it, the narrator seems entirely caught up in his own fantasy. But there is a moment late in the sequence when he realizes how fragile his fantasy is and how much protection it needs if it is not to fall immediately into crass human reality. Sometimes, before sleeping, Albertine takes off her kimono and leaves it on a chair. The narrator tells us that she keeps 'all her letters' in a pocket of that robe. Needless to say, the narrator is 'gripped by a burning curiosity' at the thought of this trove and convinced that 'the whole secret of her life lay there for the taking' (P 63). He doesn't touch the kimono, though, and doesn't look at the letters. He prefers the silence of the sleeping Albertine to whatever the talkative correspondence might have told him. And with this abstention he abandons the dream of peace and perfection he has been concocting and says the pleasure of watching Albertine wake up is even greater than that of watching her sleep—or at least is experienced as taking 'an intenser and more mysterious form' (P 64) because it is the pleasure of having her living with him: Profonde Albertine qui se réveillait quand même. This is almost too sane to be true and leaves us wondering what to do with the long analysis of the superiority of sleep when it comes to a love affair.

We have returned, by what Joyce would call a commodious vicus of recirculation, to the late sentence about sleeping and dying and unsurprisingly find that, if there are many elements of death in the perspective we are offered on sleep, there is a stubborn life of suffering in almost every thought of death. As so often in Proust, a thought that is heading in one direction turns round suddenly, as if it had forgotten something and had to go back for it.

The theme of the long paragraph that ends with this sentence is the theme of the book itself, both the book we are reading and the one the narrator has now found a way of writing. Time evaporates, he says, but past years are not separated from us. Even at this moment, in the midst of a Paris soirée, he can still hear the sound of his parents' footsteps as they accompanied Swann to the garden gate, the sound of the gate's little bell that told the child his mother would soon by with him. 'I [...] heard the very sounds themselves, heard them even though they were situated so far away in the past' (FT 356). This is the secret of the novel in waiting, but the narrator is 'frightened' to think about it because he himself is the repository of this time:

> For me still to be able to hear the tinkling there must have been no break in continuity, I must not have ceased for a moment, not taken a rest from existing, from thinking, from being conscious of myself, because this moment from long ago still stuck to me, so that I could still find it again, still go back to it.
>
> (FT 356)

And then the track changes, that is, continues on its way but also changes radically. Memories inhabit human bodies. We are close to the sense of a phrase the narrator utters just after he has heard about Albertine's death: 'our memory of a moment is not informed of everything that has happened since, the moment which it registered still lives on and, with it, the person whose form was sketched within it' (F 445).

In the late passage, the narrator continues:

> And it is because they contain [. . .] every hour of the past that human bodies can do so much damage to those who love them, because they contain so many memories of joys and desires already effaced from their minds, but cruel indeed for anyone who contemplates and projects back through the array of time the cherished body of which he is jealous, so jealous as to wish for its destruction.
>
> (FT 356–357)

We are a long way from the bliss of the madeleine and the other magical experiences of involuntary memory, real as they too are. Here, Proust's narrator is shifting from memories that inhabit him to the memories he finds in other bodies, that are inseparable from them and that are also involuntary: we can't not think of the pain that went with this waking life, and our jealousy will not die.

And now the writer—both Proust and his narrator, I take it—offers what is supposed to be a consolation but doesn't feel like one:

> For, after death, Time leaves the body, and the memories—so indifferent, so pale now—are effaced from her who no longer existed and soon will be from him whom at present they still torture, but in whom they will eventually die, when the desire of a living body is no longer there to support them. The depths of Albertine, whom I saw sleeping, and who was dead.
>
> (FT 357)

We are looking, I believe, at two of Proust's favourite thoughts, treated as if they were one and continuous with each other. As indeed they are—in time. The first is that life itself is synonymous

77

with anguish—we can hide or repress this fact, but we can't make it go away. What the narrator says of Swann is, for Proust, a sort of universal truth. 'The feeling that the person you love is in a place of enjoyment where you are not, where you cannot follow' (WS 33) is the incarnation of love itself, and it is because the person has a body that place and time can take her from you while leaving her much too close to forget. But that body will die and so will ours. So do all loves, even without physical extinction, as Proust repeatedly tells us. This removes the problem of jealousy, gets rid of the anguish. But the price is terrible. Nothing is worse than to know, even at the most intense moments of an affair, that one day you will feel nothing for this person. The death of feeling is worse than corporeal death because you have to survive it. Albertine didn't, but this is the lesson she leaves.

III

In a practical sense, the untranslatable does not exist. We can always translate badly, just as what we call the unthinkable has usually been thought, if not enacted, by many people. But there are two types of untranslatability that are relevant for any reading of Proust since they apply to hundreds, perhaps thousands of his words and sentences. Both types involve the idea of not leaving language alone. In the first case, we keep coming back to it; in the second, we feel it won't work without our help.

The philosopher Barbara Cassin wittily describes the untranslatable as 'that which we do not stop (not) translating', a permanent work in progress [2]. There is something utopian about such a notion, and we can see why publishers can't afford to think about it too often. And yet Cassin's definition could be seen as a description of any intense and imaginative reading: we are never done with it, we rework the text in our heads, we paraphrase, playfully or not. With the other type of untranslatability, we turn translation into a kind of gloss because we feel it won't work on its own: a correct translation is possible but not enough; the translator has to step in as an explainer.

'Profonde Albertine', as we have seen, is a good example of the perfectly translatable and the untranslatable in the first sense. If we are professional translators, we do the job and get paid. If we are amateur translators or just readers, we probably shuffle the meanings of the words in our heads every time we see them. Another sentence relating to Albertine and the way the narrator feels about her reads, 'Comme la souffrance va plus loin en psychologie que la psychologie' [3], literally, 'How much further suffering goes in psychology than psychology.' Scott Moncrieff has 'How much further does anguish penetrate in psychology than psychology itself' [4]. Peter Collier has 'How much more sharply suffering probes the psyche than does psychology' (F 387). We see at once why the translators feel the need to offer these miniature essays. But then the proposition is opaque in French too, and the double uninflected use of the single word is interesting. I find myself inventing, by analogy, sentences like 'In matters of justice, how much further mercy goes than justice'—I borrow the thought from Malcolm Bull's remarkable book on mercy [5]. Or, looking back to the old literary wars, 'Even in theory, practice works better than theory.' In each case, there is a discipline, a topic, an academic arena, and there is a lived experience that not only differs from that category but also is capable of transforming it on its own terms.

My sense is that Proust is not only making a claim of this kind in his enigmatic sentence but also pursuing it throughout the whole volume, called *Albertine disparue* in some editions, *La Fugitive* in others. No one will be surprised to learn that the narrator uses the word 'souffrance' twice as many times in this volume as in any other, even if the count is pretty high everywhere. This book is the strangest, most repetitive, most introverted work in the set. Malcolm Bowie wonders why the narrator's 'panic [. . .] should be entertained on such a lavish scale' [6]. This is not my question now, but something of the effect remains and helps us to see what it means to try and prove the truth of the aphorism about suffering. You have to get into deep intellectual trouble even to begin to show that it might be true.

What Proust's narrator is offering in this volume is both a detailed description of the work of repression and a vivid evocation of the repressed material. Immediately after writing his phrase about suffering, he tells us that he had thought that he wanted Albertine to leave him: 'that I no longer wanted to see her, that I no longer loved her'. Yet, hearing the words 'Miss Albertine has left', he is baffled by 'such pain' that he has to rethink everything. Or he would if his frightened self didn't have another plan. He tells himself, 'with all the good will that we lavish on those we love', that he doesn't have to take Albertine's departure too seriously. 'None of this is of any importance, because I shall get her to return straight away' (F 387).

In this delusive mood, the narrator reads Albertine's farewell note as a sort of ploy: 'She does not believe a word of all this, she has obviously written it only in order to make a scene, to frighten me' (F 389). Swann appears, appropriately here, as part of the story about anguish but also as a reminder of the narrator's delusion—Swann couldn't marry Odette when he loved her but only long after that love had died: 'What Albertine wanted was for me to stop behaving intolerably towards her, and above all, like Odette with Swann in former times—for me to decide to marry her' (F 390). This is what the narrator calls the hypothesis offered by his reason. And even when everything else in him and around him cries out how wrong it is, calling up his 'other hypothesis', the one more faithful to the anxious worry that has defined his whole relation with Albertine, he has tremendous difficulty in letting the first hypothesis go. Because it is reasonable and because reason, in this context, is a kindly, lying nurse, a sort of protective mother or grandmother.

The narrator tells himself that Albertine will return 'that very evening' since he has asked (commandeered) his friend Robert de Saint-Loup to find her and bring her back. The narrator will buy her a yacht and a Rolls Royce since she likes that kind of thing, and all will be well. But he still zig-zags between what he fears—that Albertine will never return—and his crazy attempts to pretend he has nothing to fear, and this pattern climaxes in an extraordinary letter he writes to Albertine and his own amazing interpretation of it. The narrator himself writes of a 'psychopathological universe' (F 425).

The sequence starts with a telegram from Albertine saying the narrator's employment of Saint-Loup was 'ridiculous'. 'If you needed me, my dear, why did you not write directly to me? I would have been only too pleased to return' (F 420). The narrator is reassured but unsurprisingly decides he doesn't need to rush the happy reunion. He wants to think again and makes this clear by an interesting but largely irrelevant excursus on the contrast between live human interactions and writing letters. Then he records for us the letter he sent to Albertine.

He says he is grateful to her for offer to return, but he doesn't need her. She has 'taken a decision which seems to be very wise'. In fact, the timing of her departure was perfect because if she had stayed he would have asked her to marry him, and they would have been miserable ever after. He also mentions the Rolls Royce and the yacht she is not going to have and closes by saying 'Farewell for ever' (F 422, 424).

The self-portrait now becomes perverse in its lucidity and would be comic if irony could live anywhere in this psychopathological universe: 'The likely result of my letter seemed to me [. . .] to be to make Albertine return as soon as possible. I felt greatly soothed as I wrote the letter.' Then, the narrator adds, 'But at the same time I had not ceased to weep while I was writing it,' And, in another twist, 'Since the effect of this letter seemed certain to me, I regretted having sent it' (F 425). And all of this thinking and feeling, quite dizzyingly, comes earlier in time but later in textual space—the introductory sentence is, 'But I predicted none of this'—than a passage suggesting exactly the opposite: Albertine will read the letter as the narrator unconsciously fears she will, as a sign of his irremediable need, of his monotonous, suspicious anguish, of what he himself calls his intolerable behaviour, and she will not return for that reason. 'I should have stopped to wonder', he says (F 425).

There would soon be nothing to wonder about. Albertine dies in a horse-riding accident. This is chance, rather than psychology, but a chance that feels like fate and that, like all chances in fiction, is prescribed by an author. A little more fencing occurs before this, though. Albertine replies to the narrator's letter, agreeing that they 'were destined to part' and offering to cancel the purchase of the Rolls Royce if he will tell her the name of his agent. The narrator responds to this with a crude piece of attempted blackmail: he has decided to marry Albertine's friend Andrée instead. The narrator receives two more letters from Albertine, written very shortly before her death. In the first, she says it's a wonderful idea for him 'to invite Andrée into your home'—we note she doesn't mention marriage—and says she will do anything to help persuade her friend to accept, if she needs persuading. In the second, she says, 'Would it be too late for me to return to you? If you have not yet written to Andrée, would you agree to take me back? I shall be bound by your decision [. . .] If it were favourable, I would take the next train' (F 445). There was no next train for Albertine. The blackmail was working in its way though, and, as we have seen, once a person is dead, there is a whole new life to be thought about.

IV

It is striking that the representation of homosexuality in *A la recherche* is so largely a matter of surveillance and voyeurism. The narrator as a child looks through the window of a house in the country to watch two women insulting a photograph of the father of one of them; some time later, the narrator learns his first lessons about homosexuality by watching the behaviour of two men in a Paris courtyard; in the last volume, he stands at a peephole in the wall of a male brothel to see what is happening in the next room. But then, on reflection, we note that this is how heterosexuality is portrayed too, through the stories of other people's affairs and the narrator's anxious desire to know what Albertine is up to at all times. He watches her sleep, but he would love to watch her awake, to check every minute she is away from him. Love in this novel, as we have seen, is a matter not of pleasure but of complete, notional, unavailable possession. This is exactly what the narrator himself says, commenting in the midst of an account of one of his interrogations of Albertine: 'There must be something inaccessible in what we love, something to pursue; we love only what we do not possess' (P 355).

Given this doctrine, we should, perhaps, not be surprised to find that the most frequently referenced depths of Albertine in A la recherche are the ones the narrator most wants to see as shallows: her casual sexual dalliances with other women. A curious effect of the persistence of this view is to separate the narrator and his author more clearly on these occasions than the writing does in the passages we have been looking at. The diligent suspicions of the jealous narrator, as distinct from his later desperation, are closer to nightmare comedy than to any kind of sentimental or psychological romance. We could think of this distinction as a divide between the narrator's earlier and later selves, but the distance here seems greater than that, seems to imply a more knowing, ironic mind. The narrator writes (Proust sets him up to write) that 'in leaving Balbec I had thought I that was leaving Gomorrah behind, that I was tearing Albertine away from it; alas! Gomorrah was dispersed to the four corners of the Earth' (P 16). A touch of exaggeration? Whenever the same suspicion comes up, which is often, we have the same feeling of a man looking for trouble and finding it.

The shift from pathology to comedy (and the proof of their kinship) is at its clearest in a conversation the narrator has with Albertine about literature. The narrator associates narrative patterns in

Thomas Hardy with recurring motifs in the music of Vinteuil, and from there slides quickly to Vinteuil's role as the composer of 'the national anthem of Swann's and Odette's love' and the fact that Albertine knew their daughter, Gilberte. The narrator asks, as casually as he can, 'Didn't she try to have an affair with you?' Albertine laughs and says, 'she gave me a lift once, I think, and she kissed me'. And then, 'She suddenly asked me if I liked women.' The narrator, like a detective or a philosopher, finds a contradiction between the precision of this memory and the fact that Albertine only thinks she had received a lift, but he is clearly not ready for what Albertine says next: 'I don't know why, I wanted to play a joke on her, I said yes [. . .] But we didn't do anything. She took me home like that four or five times, maybe a bit more, that's all.' A possible once has become four or five unqualified occasions, and the whole set-up would look murky to the least suspicious observer, but the narrator is very disciplined. He says, 'I had great difficulty in not asking her further questions, but, restraining myself so as not to seem to attach any importance to the matter, I came back to Hardy's stone-cutters' (P 347–348).

It doesn't occur to the narrator (although surely it does to Proust and perhaps to the narrator's older self) that Albertine is deliberately teasing him. He thinks she is ineptly failing to cover her tracks, but then this response returns to the real depths invoked by her presence and the thought of her. The narrator wants to believe in her innocence and can't give up that longing. At the same time, he can't give up his suspicions because if they vanished he wouldn't love her. In this muddled sense, he is ideally situated. In Le temps retrouvé, a year or so after Albertine's death, he even invents a new form of memory to suggest the persistence of his preoccupations. 'My memory, even my involuntary memory, had lost all recollection of the love of Albertine. But it seems there is an involuntary memory of the limbs [. . .] One's legs and arms are full of torpid memories' (FT 5). And not just of the limbs, after all, since within a page or so the narrator is asking Gilberte 'whether Albertine had loved women' and producing subtle (and probably deluded) explanations for what had been going on generally. Perhaps Albertine was innocent all along, just trying to impress him, 'to appear more experienced than she really was, and to dazzle me with the glamour of her perversity' (FT 13–14).

This clever uncertainty, a sort of final stranding of the mind, matches many themes in the novel, but there is a variant, not present in any of the published versions of the complete work, which ends the story differently. This development may not settle the matter entirely, but it certainly makes it seem as if chance, in the shape of Marcel Proust, is offering the narrator a bleak closure he may not want.

In 1986, a lost typescript of *Albertine disparue* was found, radically different from the text published in 1925 and the versions that appeared many times after. It cuts the first four sentences (including the aphorism about suffering and psychology) and, more dramatically, reduces the volume to less than half of its former length. What is most relevant here, though, is the insertion of a detail into the telegram announcing Albertine's death and a shocked reflection on that detail. The insertion simply mentions a river, so that 'while out riding' becomes 'while out riding along the banks of the Vivonne ("au bord de la Vivonne")'. 'These words', the narrator says, 'added something more atrocious to my despair' (*Albertine* 111–112).

'It cannot be a coincidence', he says—literally, 'the coincidence cannot be fortuitous'—that Albertine died near Montjouvain, the location of the house where the narrator had glimpsed his earliest scene of sadism and where Mlle Vinteuil, the organizer of the insult to the father, still lived. What was Albertine doing riding her horse in that neighbourhood? There can only be one answer. The narrator had, long before, asked Albertine about Mlle Vinteuil. She had said, 'I never had any relationship with her, I swear it' (P 366). He thought she was lying then but desperately wanted to think otherwise. Now, 'this Vivonne unintentionally confessed in the telegram' (*Albertine* 112) from Albertine's aunt finally proves, of course, that she really had been lying all the time. It offers a magical confirmation of all the suspicions he kept thinking he might get rid of.

Nathalie Mauriac Dyer, the editor of the published typescript, repeatedly calls this passage a 'capital addition'—we might think of capital punishment—and she is right (*Albertine* 12, 13, 15). We are close to the world of Dickens here, a literary domain where an author, rather than a character, arranges events and then expresses surprise at what has happened. As Proust himself does in *Le Temps retrouvé* when he introduces four extraordinary memory moments in quick succession and says, 'It seemed as if the signs [. . .] were intent on multiplying themselves' (FT 176). That's certainly how it would seem if the signs had any choice. With the capital addition, Proust introduces into the story of Albertine's death the person who is the novel's goddess of lesbianism and defies everyone, including the younger and older narrator and the patient reader, to believe this is not a conclusive omen. Comme la certitude, we might say, va plus loin en souffrance que la souffrance.

6

Proust's Law School

I

Proust did actually go to law school. He obtained a *licence* from the Paris Faculté de Droit in 1893. It's true that he quickly moved on to philosophy and received his degree in that subject two years later. Then he took up a life of moneyed leisure—until he became the writer he feared he wasn't going to be.

I don't think the formal study of the law left any major marks on Proust's writing, but I do want to suggest that there is much to be gained from seeing his work as, among other things, an intense, speculative exploration of certain kinds of crime and punishment. When the narrator of *A la recherche* tells us that he doesn't believe in justice, we are likely at first to assume that he doesn't believe in injustice either. But that is not the case. He believes passionately in injustice, finds evidence of it all around him; sees no sign anywhere of its absent, idealized counterpart. He allows one exception to this rule, as we shall see, but it is a very strange affair.

The first use of the word 'crime' in *A la recherche* concerns the attempted doings of a character in a medieval legend that the narrator has been watching in the form of a magic lantern show. 'Golo's crimes', he says, 'drove me to examine my own conscience more scrupulously', although he doesn't tell us anything about the objects of his less scrupulous concern (WS 14). Golo is the villain in the mediaeval story of Geneviève de Brabant. Her husband goes off to war, his intendant Golo makes a pass at her, and when she turns him down, orders two servants to take her (and her child) into the forest and kill them. The appointed killers decide just to abandon them instead, and mother and child are saved by a kindly female deer.

Jean-Pierre Richard shows us how Proust repeatedly associates medieval French legends with 'a phantasmagoria of crime': 'There is truly nothing more horrible, at least for some people (and we know Proust was one of them), more upsetting, more sensually moving, than a murdered child' [1]. 'Sensually moving' is a bit of a surprise but perhaps matches the narrator's connection of his conscience to the actions of Golo and certainly matches his attention to the medium of the magic lantern, which shows that figure not only as an untouchable supervillain but also as the heroic conqueror of mere three-dimensional space:

> Moving at the jerky pace of his horse, Golo [. . .] advanced jolting towards the castle of poor Geneviève de Brabant [. . .] And nothing could stop his slow ride. If the lantern was moved, I could make out Golo's horse continuing to advance over the window curtains, swelling out with their folds, descending into their fissures. The body of Golo himself, in its essence as supernatural as that of his mount, accommodated every material obstacle, every hindersome object that he encountered by taking it as his skeleton and absorbing it into himself, even the doorknob he immediately adapted to and floated invincibly over with his red robe or his pale face as noble and as melancholy as ever, but revealing no disturbance at this transvertebration.
>
> (WS 14)

Is this how the narrator wants to feel about the crimes he hasn't committed yet and perhaps never will?

David Ellison says, 'the characters of the *Recherche* do not engage in evil activity or commit crimes' [2]. This is true if we exempt various military men and politicians caught up in the Dreyfus Case and the narrator himself in his queasier moments. But metaphors of crime are everywhere in the novel, and they often act as unfulfilled prophecies, figurative expressions of what may one day find a literal life in a related form. The young woman in the story we are about to look at doesn't kill her mother, but the mother does die because of the girl's behaviour. The narrator of *A la recherche* speaks of moments when 'connecting my grandmother's death with that of Albertine, it seemed to me that my life was besmirched by a double murder' (F 463), but the language keeps him safely within the realm of seeming, even if he is talking about the dangerous topic of needing people to die so that we can understand what they meant to us.

The same trope—the murder that isn't one—finds a quietly comic life in *La Prisonnière*. The set-up is rather sly here because it involves Proust allowing one of his characters to come close to quoting him literally. Albertine has asked for a clarification of a remark. What did the narrator mean the other day when he spoke of 'the Dostoevsky side of Mme de Sévigné'? He starts to explain: 'It happens that Mme de Sévigné, sometimes, like Elstir or Dostoevsky, instead of presenting things in the logical order, that is to say starting with the cause, begins by showing us the effect, the illusion which strikes us.' Albertine interrupts to ask a supposedly naïve question. 'But did he ever murder anyone, Dostoevsky? All of his novels that I've read could be called *The Story of a Crime*' (P 350). Proust had written in a notebook in 1921 that they could all be called *Crime and Punishment* [3]. The narrator's answer is a model of hypocrisy:

> I don't think so, Albertine dear, I don't know much about his life. Certainly, like everyone else that, he had experience of sin in one form or another, probably in a form punished by the law.
>
> (P 350)

Then, he needs to distance himself a little more; he can't have dear Albertine—he literally says 'ma petite Albertine'—thinking crime is within ordinary human range:

> I do admit that Dostoevsky's preoccupation with murder has something extraordinary about it that makes me feel very remote from him [. . .] I feel as far away as possible from all that, unless there are parts of me that I don't know about [. . .]
>
> (P 351)

The narrator's denial of any affinity with the imagined Dostoevsky is truly grotesque, an effect interestingly underlined if we turn for a moment to Jacqueline Rose's novel *Albertine* and the heroine's perspective on her gaoler: 'Whatever the cost, whatever the evidence, there had to be a sexual crime' [4].

As we have seen, metaphors for Proust, far from being illustrations of a proposition made in other terms, can be analytic instruments, versions of lighting or angles of attention. The effect of this practice when Proust applies it to justice and the law is to make us wonder what happens if we remove precedent, practice, balance, and common sense from our considerations of these concepts. We seem to be left with guilt and fear of guilt, to be studied as a form of social psychology, or psychological sociology, that much resembles Foucault's idea of an altered mode of understanding.

Its truths are not on the surface or entire; we have to look for them underground or reassemble them from their fragments.

II

In the story 'Confession d'une jeune fille', published in *Les Plaisirs et le jours* (1896), a young woman believes she has killed her mother by having sex with a young man who is not her fiancé. Or perhaps by something more subtle: she failed to erase the visual sign of her pleasure in the act: 'I would have preferred my mother to see me commit yet other crimes—or even that particular one, but without her catching sight of the expression of joy that my face had in the mirror' (PD 65).

The young woman is unnamed and speaks in the first person, as we have seen. She is writing to us, to a page, to herself, to no one. After her mother's death, she tried to kill herself and failed, though she was fatally wounded and has been given eight days to live. All she can do, she says, is to 'strive to grasp the whole horrible chain of circumstances'. She is fond of the word 'crime'. She says she 'was committing the greatest of crimes against my mother'; 'No one suspected the secret crime of my life' (PD 105, 113).

These words, and many other items of the young woman's language, cry out—too loudly perhaps—for psychoanalytic attention. What we might call sexual awakening she calls 'all the predispositions towards evil that, like all children of my age (and in those days no more than them) I bore within me'. Those days end when she hangs out with a male cousin of fifteen—she herself is fourteen at the time—who is 'extremely prone to vice' and teaches her things that made her 'shudder with remorse and pleasure'—that last mixture seems to have come straight out of

Poe or Baudelaire. But then the parents must have played a role here. Where else would the girl have got her idea of vice from? The soon-to-be-murdered mother especially has to be part of the problem because she doesn't know how to manage her affection and her idea of discipline for the child. She has her 'severities', the daughter says, and speaks of her mother's 'unyielding sense of justice', which sounds like very bad news (PD 107).

Her mother was in the habit of leaving the girl to stay with her uncles in the country and made only brief visits, 'the sweetest and yet cruellest things', the girl says:

> During those two days she would lavish on me an affection of which she was usually very chary [. . .] She would come and say goodnight to me in my bed, an old habit she had otherwise given up, since it gave me too much pleasure and too much pain.
>
> (PD 106)

The girl understands that these moments of tenderness are the ones where her mother is 'really herself' and that 'her habitual frigidity must be something she imposed on herself with an effort'. But then why the effort? Because she believes the girl is already spoiled by kindness and, above all, needs to acquire the discipline she chronically lacks. She needs willpower or she is lost: 'What made my mother so sad was my lack of willpower. I did everything on a momentary impulse.' The girl herself buys entirely into this mythology, and the self-fulfilling consequence hardly needs a prophecy. 'To desire strength of will was not enough. I would have needed to do just what I could not do without strength of will: will it' (PD 106, 110). It's as if the girl has been reading, as Proust certainly had, a book much consulted at the time, Théodule Ribot's *Maladies de la volonté* (1883). Or, indeed, has been reading Proust's stories of the goodnight kiss.

But this is all background. When the girl turns sixteen she falls in love with a 'perverse and spiteful' boy and improves on her earlier lessons from her cousin. She feels an 'agonized remorse' at first, but her friends persuade her that she is only doing what young girls do, and, in any case, how is she supposed to manage morality if she doesn't have any willpower? She plans to change her ways but only acquires a new vice: procrastination. This is where she starts to talk of crime—she also speaks of 'the suicide' of her mind—and builds the paradox she will escape from only through death. The more she betrays her mother's hopes, the more respectfully she behaves towards her: she is regarded as 'the ideal young girl' (PD 111, 113).

Her story moves on four years. She thinks 'necessity' will take over the task of the still absent will and accepts as her future husband the first young man her mother mentions to her. He sounds like a plausible solution: he is extremely intelligent, gentle, and energetic. The girl confesses her sins to her priest and asks him if she should tell her fiancé. The priest is kind enough to say no but asks her to swear that she 'would never relapse into those errors', and she is happy to do this (PD 114). Her mother's health is failing, a fact that can't really be separated from this redemptive moment, and, curiously enough, the mother's health revives as the girl's virtue flourishes. The congruence would represent rather crude plotting if Proust didn't lend the girl a sort of intuition about what kind of story she is in. There is 'a mysterious solidarity' between mother and daughter, 'despite her total ignorance of my misdeeds' (PD 114). The doctors say she just needs a couple of weeks' rest, and there will be no chance of a relapse. You don't have to be a Freudian to realize this is the mother's death sentence—the girl's as well.

One evening, our heroine has a little too much to drink. The fiancé is absent, Jacques, 'the young man who bore the greatest share of responsibility for my former errors', is present at dinner, and the obvious event ensues. Afterwards, the girl looks at herself in the mirror. Jacques' face joins hers there and both reflect 'a sensual, stupid and brutal joy' and none of the anguish the girl, at least, is feeling. Then she sees something else:

> On the balcony, outside the window, I saw my mother gazing at me, horror-struck. I don't know if she cried out, I heard nothing, but she fell backwards and remained with her head caught between the two bars of the railing.
>
> (PD 115)

She is scarcely able to think of her mother's death. The question is: did her mother see that expression? The young woman can't avoid the question, but she can accept only one answer. 'No, she can't possibly have seen it. It was a coincidence [...] She was struck down by apoplexy a minute before she saw me [. . .] She didn't see that expression' (PD 118). The girl committed her crime not because she had to, or because of any inherent probability, but because the imagination of crime required her to, as well as the fidelity of fiction to its own ends, to what we might call the writer's will.

III

Proust's mother, Jeanne Proust née Weil, died in September 1905 as a result of an uremic crisis. There were no suspicious circumstances; there was no legal inquiry. If there is such a thing as a death from natural causes, this was a clear instance. But Proust the writer and neuropath didn't believe in natural causes, for death or for many other occurrences. Or rather, he believed in cause and effect like everyone else, and he knew all too well that his mother was really dead. But he also believed that nature and logic often look too much like names for hindsight, vain, retrospective corrections of chance or alternative causalities. In one of his versions of her end, Jeanne Proust had died because her husband had died earlier, and she didn't love her son enough to stay alive for him. Such an interpretation doesn't cancel or even quarrel with natural causes, but it certainly puts them in the shade.

On 24 January 1907, in Paris, a man murdered his mother and then killed himself. He was called Henri van Blarenberghe. Two weeks after the event, Marcel Proust published an article in *Le Figaro* about the case. The article's headline, 'Filial feelings of a parricide', feels desolate and seems to announce a cruel irony rather than a paradox. 'Filial' conjures up (and then throws away) a whole mythology of the family, implying loyalty and duty, a sense of debt, an acknowledgement of time and inheritance. This is exactly where the article starts:

> When Henry van Blarenberghe's father died a few months ago I remembered that my mother had known his wife well. Since the death of my parents I am (in a sense it would be inappropriate to be more specific about here) less myself, more their son. Without turning away from my friends, I find myself turning more readily to theirs. And the letters that I write now are for the most part those that I believe they would have written, those they can no longer write and that I write in their stead, congratulations, condolences above all to friends of theirs whom I often barely know. So when Mme van Blarenberghe lost her husband, I wanted to send her an indication of the sadness my parents would have felt on the occasion.
>
> ('Sentiments' 350)

The contrast between the writer and the murderer seems complete. Their mothers knew each other, but only one of the sons feels or behaves like a son. Or rather, since Proust is about to tell us how polite the son was in responding to his letter, how full van Blarenberghe's missive was of 'a great filial love', the possessor of such proper feelings becomes, with the crime, an incomprehensible creature, driven by whatever emotions the violent perpetrator of a matricide may be taken to have. This is what the newspaper headlines said at the time, with very few exceptions: 'Drama of Madness in Paris' (*Le Petit Journal*), 'Terrible Drama of Madness' (*La Gazette de France*), 'A Madman Kills His Mother and Then Commits Suicide' (*L'Echo de Paris*). A person would have to be mad to murder his mother.

Proust's most recent interaction with van Blarenberghe occurred a couple of weeks before the crime. Proust had asked him for 'some information' about an employee of a railway line (van Blarenberghe was chairman of the administrative board) 'in whom one of my friends was interested'('Sentiments' 554, 555). The friend was probably Proust himself, and there is an interesting gay subtext here that the article doesn't pursue. Van Blarenberghe couldn't help with the information but wrote a very courteous note about his failure to do so. Proust quotes this letter and others not just as a proof of how ordinary and polite the man was and how strange and sudden crime is but as a clear sign that horror can invade any life at any time: 'This practical reasonableness seems to exclude what happened even more than the beautiful and profound sadness of the last lines do' ('Sentiments' 560). There are no such exclusions.

Moved by the last words Mme van Blarenberghe speaks before she dies—'Henri, what have you done to me?' (more literally, 'what have you made of me'—qu'as-tu fait de moi?), Proust decides that the murder represents only a violent form of the effect all sons have on their mothers. The wording is wonderfully precise, with the imagined indictment coming from the mother:

> If we wished to think about it, there is perhaps no truly loving mother who could not, in her last hours, often well before, reproach her son in this way.
>
> ('Sentiments' 560)

Then, the perspective shifts, the angle of vision becomes that of the son—or the sons, since many of us are now in it together:

> In the end, we make older, we kill everyone who loves us through the worries we cause them, through the disturbed tenderness itself that we inspire and constantly alarm. If we knew how to see in a loved body the slow labor of destruction pursued by the its painful, animated tenderness, see the withered eyes, the hair that for so long had remained unconquerably black finally defeated like the rest and going white, the hardened arteries, the blocked kidneys, the strained heart, the defeated courage in regard to life, the heavy, slowed-down walk, the mind that knows it has nothing more to hope for, when it used to reawaken so indefatigably to invincible hopes, the gaiety itself, the innate and apparently immortal gaiety, which kept company so amiably with sadness, and now dried up for ever [. . .]
>
> ('Sentiments' 560)

The person who could see this, Proust concludes, might kill himself straight away, unable to stand the horror of his life any more. As Henri van Blarenberghe did. The proposition is truly startling at this point, almost unmanageable. Of course, Proust's account of his mother's slow dying has a tenderness that is entirely lacking in van Blarenberghe's sudden act. And technically, Proust and the rest of us have committed no crime. But the technicality is just what Proust wants us to stare at and dismiss. Oscar Wilde said something very similar in the poem Proust is remembering, but Proust has altered the grammar in a striking way: not each man kills the thing he loves but each man kills the thing that loves him.

At various points in the article, Proust links the news story with Greek myth and Shakespearean tragedy, invoking the madness of Ajax, the desperate self-harming grief of Oedipus, and King Lear's incredulous gazing at his daughter's corpse. The connections are madness and violence and the family, and it is worth noting that none of these instances involves matricide: Ajax killed shepherds and sheep, thinking they were an outpost of the Trojan army; Oedipus killed his father long ago and now, at the sight of his dead mother, blinds himself; and Lear is at the bleak end of a long family quarrel. What does come up in these allusions is the idea of not being able to live with certain forms of knowledge, as in the passage I have quoted above. Ajax returns from his madness and sees what he has done and so does Henri van Blarenberghe. Proust comments, 'Sorrow (or pain) does not kill straight away, since he did not die on seeing his murdered mother before him' ('Sentiments' 557). But again, a certain kind of death is conjured up only in order for it not to happen. Van Blarenberghe doesn't die of grief; he has to kill himself laboriously, hacking at his body with a dagger and shooting himself in the head. It's the newspaper account of the man's eye hanging out on his pillow that provokes Proust's allusion to Oedipus, and 'the most terrible act that the history of human suffering has handed down to us' ('Sentiments' 558). It is important that 'history' here means 'myth' and that Proust doesn't want to make the distinction. Perhaps the history of human suffering will always have to be mythical in part.

The missing piece of the ancient assembly, the story of Orestes, the man who did actually kill his mother, showed up in the last paragraph Proust wrote for his piece, but the editor at the *Figaro* cut it. And the story itself was a little displaced anyway. Proust evoked not the killing but the aftermath, the pursuit of the matricide by the Furies, and the ultimate consecration of his tomb at Sparta as a holy place. This setting links Orestes with Oedipus since his tomb at Colonus was also a sacred spot. Nothing is more sublime than the memory of these men who killed, respectively, their mother and their father. But then the last word of the article goes not to them or to their strange consecration but to the Furies and the more immediate consequence of Orestes's act. The Furies say, 'We drive the parricidal son far from the altars' ('Sentiments' 1571).

IV

Ultimately, the Dreyfus Affair for Proust was comparable to famous literary works not for its twists and murkiness but for what he saw as its happy ending. In 1906, when Dreyfus was cleared and reinstated, Proust wrote to his friend Mme Geneviève Strauss:

> It is curious to think that for once life is behaving like a novel—as it so rarely does. Alas in these last ten years we have both had many sorrows in our lives, many disappointments, many torments. And for neither of us is the hour going to strike when our sorrows are changed into joys, our disappointments into unexpected achievements, and our torments into delicious triumphs [. . .] But this is not how it is for Dreyfus [. . .] Life has been providential for [him] in the manner of fairy-tales and romantic novels. This is because our sadnesses were based on truths, on psychological, human and

sentimental truths. [His] sufferings were based on errors. Happy
are those who are victims of judicial errors—judicial or other kinds
of errors. They are the only human beings for whom there are
revenges and reparations [...] [5].

There is surely a curious tactlessness in writing of 'delicious
triumphs' and 'happy' victims in this context or, indeed, in feeling sorry for oneself by comparison. Dreyfus certainly did not
experience his rehabilitation as any sort of victory; his life had
been drastically and permanently altered in ways that Proust and
his correspondent could not begin to imagine. But the wording is
emblematic of a whole region of Proust's thought.

This region is best represented, I think, by a strange claim Proust
has his narrator make in one of the last volumes of *A la recherche
du temps perdu*. Albertine has taken off to her aunt's place in the
country and, within seventy pages or so, will die in a horse-riding
accident. The narrator who was untranslatably discussing suffering now reflects uncannily on justice. At one point, he speaks of
himself as 'the most lax and yet most vulnerable of policemen',
meaning he has been unable to follow up on his old systematic
surveillance of Albertine (F 402). He used almost to take satisfaction in his astuteness, he says. He was 'like a murderer who
knows he cannot be found out, but who is afraid and suddenly
sees the name of his victim written at the head of a file on the desk
of the examining magistrate who has summoned him to appear'
(F 399).

To complete the picture, we need to add the narrator's brush
with the non-metaphorical police. He picks up a young girl on the
street, takes her home, sits her on his knee, finds the experience is
not cheering him up, and sends her away with 500 francs—a lot
of money and, in anyone else's eyes, already suspicious. This is all

creepy enough, although the narrator seems to think this is one of the few normal things he's done since Albertine left. He just wants company, he says, 'the succour of an innocent presence'. However, not everyone thinks such games are innocent, and some time later the narrator is summoned to the local police station because of a complaint from the girl's parents, an accusation of 'seducing a minor' (F 400, 411).

At the police station, the narrator meets the girl's parents and gets a telling off from the chief of police, although as soon as the parents are gone, the same chief tells him to be more careful next time and to consider that, for that kind of money, he could do much better. The chief himself is a fellow 'who had a weakness for little girls', although we are not told how the narrator knows this (F 412). When he gets home, he discovers that a policeman has been talking to his maid Françoise and the concierge, both of whom, thinking of Albertine, say yes, the master is in the habit of bringing girls home. Now he definitely feels tagged by justice, and tells us that:

> suddenly, in a moment of unwitting confusion (for in fact I had never thought that Albertine, being over the age of consent, was allowed to live with me, even to be my mistress), it seemed that 'the seduction of minors' could also refer to Albertine. Thus my life seemed walled in on all sides. And at the thought that I had not lived a chaste life with her, I found in the punishment inflicted upon me for having cradled an unknown little girl in my arms the balance which almost always occurs in human punishment, suggesting that there is hardly ever either a just condemnation or a judicial error but a kind of harmony between the false notion of an innocent act entertained by the judge and the culpable actions of which he is unaware.
>
> (F 414)

Commenting on this passage, Antoine Compagnon says the thought is 'indeed dreadful'. 'The arbitrariness of human justice', Compagnon continues, 'is counterbalanced by Evil in the absolute': 'In short, there is always a crime to punish' [6]. This is certainly true in the phrase from Joseph de Maistre that Proust is partly paraphrasing and partly extending. De Maistre says that 'it is [. . .] possible that someone sentenced for a crime he has not committed has really deserved this sentence for another absolutely unknown crime' [7]. It is possible, of course, but the question is who would want to entertain this possibility and why? In de Maistre's perspective, it is fundamentally a religious, otherworldly suggestion and similar in spirit to Dostoevsky's sense of these matters. Dmitri Karamazov says, 'I am not guilty of my father's blood! I accept punishment not because I killed him, but because I wanted to kill him, and might well have killed him [. . .]' [8]. But he didn't kill him, and Dmitri, while accepting his symbolic punishment, fights his case legally and insists on his real innocence.

Proust's proposition, unlike de Maistre's, goes two ways. Where de Maistre's perspective is religious, Proust's is resolutely secular and manages, at the same time, to be both sceptical (about human justice) and superstitious (about human guilt). Hardly any legal verdict is just, and hardly any judicial error is wrong. This is not so much a proposition about the law as a fantasy of a horrible double near-perfection. There are plenty of judicial errors, nothing but judicial errors. But no error is only an error because, in some ghastly dimension of moral harmony, all errors turn out to be displaced instances of justice.

Proust's narrator is certainly not aware of the lamentable comedy in his thought, where his petty supposed innocence ('What's wrong with messing around with little girls?') and his petty sup-posed offence ('Albertine and I were not even married') lead directly into Dostoevskyan darkness and metaphysical reflec-tions on justice. The Dreyfus Case flickers here too since *Une erreur judiciaire* was the name of the first book about it. But then the lapse seems even more shallow: is our man really comparing a small embarrassment at the police station to five years on Devil's Island?

The answer is that he scarcely knows what he is doing, as we have seen; and his failure of tact and sense of proportion are also symptoms of his condition. But he is not saying nothing. Scepti-cism about justice, hyperbolically expressed in the form 'there is almost never a just verdict', was a reasonable stance in the time of Dreyfus and has been a reasonable stance in countries and times much closer to us—as Louis Begley's book about Dreyfus suggests. And a fantasy of displaced but unerring justice ('there is almost never a judicial error') may represent not the sinister view that evil is everywhere but the charmed view that a non-existent God knows all my secrets. This view is not reasonable, like the scepticism about justice, but it is intelligible, and I'm sure many of us have subscribed to a version of it at some time or other. But it's not a proposition about God or about the law. It's a dramatization of the notion of guilt.

This, finally perhaps, was how Proust saw the fairy tale of Alfred Dreyfus. Dreyfus escaped, through someone else's error, through his country's error, the devastating truths not only of the sorrows and disappointments of ordinary people but also of the whole precarious, provisional, and unstable social world that came to be associated with his name. Marcel Thomas reminds us that Alfred Dreyfus was the man who knew least about the Dreyfus

Affair—he was away at the time. But we could put the matter another way. Dreyfus always, quite correctly, saw his case from the point of view of innocence, while Proust, in spite of his faith in Dreyfus's literal innocence, imagined it from the point of view of guilt. That was how he imagined all cases, and that is why he understood Dreyfus's world better than Dreyfus did.

Is this a little paranoid? Yes. But we may wish to recall Adorno's aphorism in *Minima Moralia* about the relation of paranoia to reality. I like to think he learned this lesson in Proust's law school:

> Psychology knows that he who imagines disasters in some way desires them. But why do they come so eagerly to meet him? Something in reality strikes a chord in paranoid fantasy and is warped by it [9].

7

After the Ball

I

A *la recherche du temps perdu* ends on two long-planned scenes—there were drafts as early as 1908 and 1909. The first involves a quadruple repeat of the memory experience associated with the taste of a madeleine in the first volume and a long meditation on the consequences of this confirmation; the second centres on what Proust's narrator calls 'un coup de théâtre', an event that threatens all the hopes the first set of scenes had resurrected: 'In fact, as soon as I entered the great drawing-room [...] a dramatic turn of events occurred which seemed to raise the gravest objections to my undertaking' (FT 229).

The narrator faces these objections 'at the very moment when I wanted to begin to clarify, to intellectualize within a work of art, realities whose nature was extra-temporal' (FT 239). The logic here is a little too pure, too intelligent, in Proust's terms. The narrator was not going to write about extra-temporal realities but about another sort of time, the time that passes and comes back, as distinct from just passing. But his distress is obviously real, and the apparent contradiction is all the more difficult for being messy. It also makes the ongoing mockery of the self and the world all the funnier.

The 'coup de théâtre' is this. The narrator has been alone in his host's library, waiting for a recital to end so he can join the other guests. He has been away from Paris for the last few years, making only a couple of short visits, so this is effectively his return to high society. He enters the drawing-room and, for a moment, doesn't recognize his host or any of the guests. They appear to be in disguise, powdered, dressed up in white beards and moustaches. He hadn't realized that the soirée was a fancy-dress ball. The Prince de Guermantes is dragging his feet like someone taking part in an allegory representing the 'Ages of Life'. One of the guests has covered his face with so many wrinkles and his eyelashes protrude so visibly that he must be playing a role. The narrator says he tries to ignore the 'travesty' involved here but wonders whether he ought rather to congratulate the guests on the success of their impersonations.

He really goes to town on an old enemy, Monsieur d'Argencourt. This figure has not only fitted himself out with 'an extraordinary beard of improbable whiteness' but has also turned his usual stiff, impressive solemnity into the posture of 'an old beggar', has become 'a decrepit old man' with trembling limbs and a fixed, stupid smile. The narrator laughs wildly at this 'sublime dodderer' (FT 230, 231) and compares Argencourt's 'extraordinary number' to that of an actor at the end of his career and then wonders whether the actor is quite the right image. Perhaps a puppet would be better. He imagines the man as taking part:

> in a scientific and philosophical puppet-show, in which he served, as in a funeral address or a lecture at the Sorbonne, both as a reminder of the vanity of things and as a specimen of natural history.
>
> (FT 233)

The narrator is insisting too much, and the joke is on him as well as by him. He has been away, but he would have needed several decades to meet, in reality, with the effect he is describing. Of course, he is evoking and animating something else: his own denial of time, his ridiculous surprise. These people are older and probably would have looked older earlier if the narrator had been seeing them in something like the current light. And they are not as old as he now pictures them because no one is; the whole theatre is a refraction of his lavish amazement.

As so often in Proust, the joke amuses us in two modes. It is witty, elaborate, and unmistakably some kind of caricature. Then it is pushed a little further, dwelt on, and becomes funny in a different way because it begins to look inept, outstaying its welcome, moving towards cliché. This is especially true when the narrator finds himself caught in a more literal expression of time. He runs into the Duchesse de Guermantes at the party, and she introduces him to another guest as her oldest friend. He should have been flattered. He was her acquaintance, perhaps even a protégé, and he had known her a long time. But he had 'never for a moment thought I might be one of her friends' (FT 236). Right now, though, he just feels unhappy: how could he be old?

A few moments later, someone calls him 'an old Parisian', and, moments after that, he receives a note from someone who signs himself as 'your young friend'. The narrator is indignant: 'That was how I used to write to people who were thirty years older than myself.' The narrator himself draws our attention to the pile-up of bad signs, asserting that the fact of his own aging 'was [. . .] proclaimed by successive remarks which every few minutes assailed my ears like the trumpets of Judgment Day' (FT 236, 176, 235).

Things get even worse. The narrator's friend Bloch appears, although the narrator thinks, for a moment, that this figure may be his friend's father. Then he recognizes the changes in the younger Bloch, who shows the 'weariness of an amiable old man'. For good measure, someone has just said that Bloch 'certainly looked his age'. This set-up produces a marvellous aphorism: 'I understood [. . .] that it is out of adolescents who last a sufficient number of years that life makes old men' (FT 237).

This particular game is not quite over. Someone asks the narrator if he is not afraid of catching the war-time flu that is raging. Another person says, 'it usually attacks younger people', and, as with the duchess's compliment, the narrator takes this consolation as another nail in his coffin. He is then told, as a last, entirely unneeded confirmation of his condition, that someone has referred to him as 'old father' so-and-so, using his actual surname. He explains, 'And as I did not have any children, it could only be an allusion to my age' (FT 237). This last bit of pedantry destroys any chance he might have had of our feeling sorry for him—Proust the author is quietly laughing at his narrator as writer and as character.

Not everything is comic here, though, and this hesitancy of mood is part of Proust's signature. No one knows better—except perhaps Dickens and Nabokov—that daily life all too often assumes the structure of farce, where a flurry of wrong bedrooms seems to summarize the whole of existence.

II

The narrator in A la recherche du temps perdu refers quite often to the text we are reading, naming 'the invisible vocation which is the subject of this book' and 'the rest of my story' (GW 395; SYG 515). He even recalls the moment of what we have seen as the hesitations of *Contre Sainte-Beuve*: His 'hopes', he says, 'were [...] doomed to frustration every time I sat down to a desk to sketch the draft of critical study or a novel' (SYG 89). Sometimes, 'this book' still seems to belong to the future. All he has to his literary credit, he says, are 'some very thin articles', adding, on another occasion, that he has published 'some studies'. He is probably being a little too modest here, in part because he trying to show how wrong those people are who mistake him for a successful, even a great writer. And he has made some sort of start on his novel because he has shown it to a few people, who didn't understand it at all. But then he also talks about what 'the final volumes of this work will show' and says, 'we have seen' what previous episodes have proved (GW 63, FT 354).

But who is talking to whom when we read these allusions to a novel in progress? As actual readers of Proust's book, we have seen or read precisely these words and many others. But then is the fictional narrator speaking to us or to his fictional audience? Do we get a little dizzy thinking about his imagining as part of the past a beginning he hasn't arrived at yet, or do we think Proust could just be making casual use of an old convention: the writer pretends she is telling a tale and readers pretend they are listening? The material acts of writing and reading are bracketed or forgotten.

When, in *Bleak House*, Esther Summerson writes of 'my portion of these pages' [1], meaning that half of the novel which is not the domain of the omniscient narrator, do we really think of her physically writing, or do we translate her portion as representing her angle on the story, a fictional division that borrows a real division of style? When David Copperfield, similarly, wonders whether he is going to be the hero of 'these pages', do we linger over the actual volume in our hands and wonder if it is a duplicate of something David has written? There is only one book here, we might think, the one written by Dickens, and David is an employee, doing a familiar, first-person job. He is also, in case we have any doubts, speaking the unspeakable, as when he says, in the first chapter title, 'I am born' [2].

I don't think we should rush to choose between our answers since both have their attractions. The old convention allows us to settle into the fiction and not worry too much about the textual or epistemological status of the characters. The second offers us Esther and David, dizzyingly, as fictional characters who know they are in a real book, like Molly Bloom at a certain moment in *Ulysses* or Proust's narrator when he casually drops his author's first name. I am, I confess, much drawn to the second view, which I take as congenital (and congenial) to fiction and not as a post-modern trope. There are more of such games in Jane Austen, for example, than in most twentieth-century writers. It is, we might say, adapting an idiom from Proust, the Nabokov side of George Eliot. But I also like the idea of an untroubled enjoyment of literary illusion, and we can, I believe, allow ourselves both postures, although perhaps not at exactly the same time.

The two postures correspond precisely to the two major views of what it is we are reading when we take on *A la recherche du temps perdu*, that is, what role we assign to the actual work. An

earlier consensus suggested that we are enjoying the very novel
the narrator says he is about to start work on and will complete if
he has time. It is not an accident (as they say) that the last sentence
of the completed work begins with, 'At least, if' and ends with
'in Time'. I will come back to this construction. Joshua Landy,
subtly contesting the consensus, takes half a page to list the distinguished critics who subscribed to it. The view is too simple
and too smooth, but sometimes we need simplicity and smooth-
ness. The chief problem with it, apart from many narratological
hitches, is that it loses sight of, or buries, at least two other serious
and moving possibilities: the narrator didn't finish his book, he
just got to the point where he thought he might; the book we are
reading, in spite of many alluring invitations to the contrary, may
be nothing like the work the narrator planned to write or could
write.

A dizzying moment—Antoine Compagnon calls it 'one of the
strangest pages in *La Recherche*' [3]—plays with all these perspectives. The narrator thinks Charles Swann should have a little more
respect for the book in which he was a major character, or at least
be more grateful for the part the work played in the diffusion of
his social fame:

> It is [. . .] because someone whom you must have considered a lit-
> tle idiot has made you the hero of one of his novels that people are
> beginning to talk about you again, and perhaps you will live on.
>
> (P 182)

This remark appears in the middle of a passage about Swann's
death—the same passage where the English words *great event* are
to be seen—so the narrator knows he is addressing a ghost. Even

so, it is a little odd for a fictional narrator to be addressing another
fictional character as an immediately identifiable historical figure,
and the strangeness continues:

> If people talk so much about the Tissot painting set on the bal-
> cony of the Rue Royale Club, where you are standing with Gallifet,
> Edmond de Polignac and Saint Maurice, it is because they can see
> there is something of you in the character of Swann.
>
> (P 182)

The painting actually exists, and a man called Charles is found
there among the other named persons. He is Charles Haas, the
chief but not the only model for the character of Swann. We can,
if we work at it, preserve some kind of realistic illusion here. The
narrator, thinking of the fictional figure who has just died, looks
far into the future when his as yet unstarted book is being read,
and he registers the imaginary ingratitude he assumes will still be
in place. Proust may be thinking here of Dostoevsky, who likes to
play similar games with the status of fiction. In *The Adolescent*, the
narrator says:

> I am not writing for publication. I'll probably have a reader only
> in some ten years, when everything is already so apparent, past
> and proven, that there will no longer be any point in blushing. And
> therefore, if I sometimes address my reader [...] it's merely a device.
> My reader is a fantastic character [4].

The easier but still quite complicated interpretation turns to
Proust himself and watches him playing games with his puppet-
narrator. The chronology in this view is perfectly coherent: the
part of *A la recherche* called *Du côté de chez Swann* was published in

1913 and a copy of the Tissot painting appeared in the magazine *L'Illustration* in 1922. The lines about Swann and the painting, Jean Milly tells us, 'are one of the last references to actuality introduced into the novel' [5]. The suggestion is, perhaps, that Haas, rather than Swann, should be grateful, but he had died in 1902 (a little later than Swann, if we follow an accepted imaginary time scheme) so also would be able to fail to present only ghostly thanks. The accent falls the more heavily on the narrator's injured vanity, his infatuation with the work he may never complete.

This sort of intricacy leads us to one of the most famous cruces in *A la recherche du temps perdu*, the moment I have mentioned when the narrator seems to know his author's name. There are actually two such moments, but one of them is only odd and the other is hallucinatory. It is true that the name 'Marcel' is 'frequent in the early drafts', as Milly says [6], and, in one of his sketches, Proust allows the narrator to evoke the missing identification. The Princesse de Guermantes (the ex-Mme Verdurin) addresses him 'by calling me by my first name' [7]. But this gesture rather advertises the general absence. And, in the end, Proust took out all of the mentions except the two we are looking at.

In a brief note to her friend, Albertine uses the name 'Marcel' three times: 'Dear darling Marcel [...] Oh Marcel, Marcel!' (P 140). There is, of course, no reason why Albertine's friend should not be called Marcel. It's a name that belongs to many people who are not Proust, and many fictional characters have the names of actual persons. There are lots of Mrs Bennetts in the historical world, and we do meet a Jane in a novel by Jane Austen.

It is strange though that only Albertine speaks the name, and the other mention also comes from her. She has been asleep and wakes to say:

> 'darling' or 'my darling', followed by my Christian name, which, if we give the narrator the same name as the author of this book, would produce 'darling Marcel' or 'my darling Marcel'.

> (P 64)

The 'we' appears in English because there is no other way of creating an idiomatic sentence (Scott Moncrieff makes the same move), but it does introduce another person into a rather crowded space. The French has only an unowned present participle, but I suppose there is a sort of otherworldly or anterior presence in the idea of giving, which the French phrase nom de baptême strongly suggests. There would be two gifts of the name in question: an ancient, actual one to Proust himself and a speculative one to the narrator. This is what the grammar says in French: en donnant au narrateur le même nom qu'à l'auteur de ce livre, 'giving to the narrator the same name as to the author of this book'. The critical consensus is that this whole intervention is a slip, or a joke, that Proust would have removed if he had had more time for his revisions. This may be true, but the wording seems too careful for a slip, and it is surely important that the whole proposition remains a possibility that is both logically deferred and materially enacted. Proust himself, it seems, doesn't want finally to give his name to his narrator or visibly to take it away. He needs this *alter ego*, who is sometimes scarcely *alter* at all and sometimes not even an *ego*. The formal distinction between the narrator and the author sounds like reader-response theory long before its time, but, of course, either of those figures could be speaking discreetly about themselves, as when one says 'your humble servant or admirer'. Jean Milly's reflection on what is happening here is very helpful:

> The narrator is, essentially, a being without a name or a face: more like a voice and an arrangement of words, those of Proust, but as *figures* and kept at a distance from the author himself [8].

III

Many endings in mortal life are just facts, hard and irreversible, a consequence of living in time. Imagined endings are often different, designed, properly timed, so to speak, refusals of mere chronology. This double proposition is the theme of Frank Kermode's wonderful book, *The Sense of an Ending,* and in a more worried mode, of one of Franz Kafka's most memorable aphorisms:

> The Messiah will come only when he is no longer necessary, he will come only after his arrival, he will come not on the last day, but on the very last [9].

It is surprisingly easy to accommodate the contradiction at the end of the sentence. Of course, our idea of lateness is inadequate; there is always something later than that. But the main interest of the proposition perhaps lies in the notion that gods too can fail to keep appointments and that notions of timing can always be rewritten. This is precisely what Proust and his narrator are doing as they seek to conclude an exploration of time that was always also a dream of its defeat.

The last page of the manuscript of *A la recherche du temps perdu* allows us to distinguish very clearly between the author and the narrator of the novel—and then watch our distinction fade as we think a little more about it. We know that the author placed the word 'end' after the closure of his text and that the narrator could not have done this since he is still talking about starting the book he is in. Or could he? Perhaps he did sign off in the fiction as a futuristic fantasy of what for Proust happened in real time.

Proust's housekeeper, Celeste Albaret, tells us that one morning in the spring of 1922 (he died in November of that year), Proust said to her that he had not only put an end to his book but had also written the key word: *'j'ai mis le mot "fin"'* [10]. Another theory suggests that he could have written these words as early as May 1919, but this possibility only enriches the mythological moment. Writing the word 'end' is not the same as finishing. A facsimile of the last manuscript page shows that although the closing words of the book, 'in time', 'dans le temps', remain the same, they are crossed out three times before being written again and left to stand. The latest added clause runs through the top of the letter F of *Fin*.

Here is what the last sentence looks like if we take it to pieces. I am following Jean-Yves Tadié's analysis [11]. The main clause is simply 'my first concern would be to mark (my work) with the seal of time and to describe the people in it as occupying a place in time'. The number of subordinate clauses rises with the revisions from three to eight (ten in French), and, above all, the giants appear, recalling Proust's metaphor of time as creating high stilts for us. Here is what is likely to have been the first version:

> if enough time was left to me to complete my work, my first concern would be to mark it with the seal of time and to describe the people in it, even at the risk of making them seem colossal and unnatural creatures, as occupying a place far larger than the very limited one reserved for them in space, a place in Time.

And here's the last, the one that trespasses on the word *fin:*

> if enough time was left to me to complete my work, my first concern would be to describe the people in it, even at the risk of making them seem colossal and unnatural creatures, as occupying a place far larger than the very limited one reserved for them in space, a place in fact almost infinitely extended, since they are in simultaneous contact, like giants immersed in the years, with such distant periods of their lives, between which so many days have taken up their place—in Time.
>
> (FT 358)

The beauty of this graphic puzzle is that it enacts a double perception. *A la recherche du temps perdu* was, in one sense, 'finished' long ago, not in 1919 but as early as 1911; that is, Proust knew where and how the story would end. Except that the book would never end because, as long as he was alive and conscious, Proust would keep writing. There would always be another subordinate clause to add, and the last sentence displays in brief what the whole novel has been doing: diligently finding room for more and more events between the first and last scenes, so that World War I and much else could be folded into an expanding but already closed imaginative circle. The Messiah came quite early and yet was still on his way. Or to quote Proust himself, 'In life novels never end' [12].

The giants may be a good note on which to fail to close this small book, too. They are too tall, they have occupied too much time, most of it wasted, but they are glamorous in their way, and, if we listen carefully, we may hear something of their impossible music:

> as if humankind were perched on top of living stilts which never stop growing, sometimes becoming taller than church steeples, until eventually they made walking difficult and dangerous, and down from which, all of a sudden, they fall [...] I began to be afraid that the stilts on which I myself was standing had already reached that height [...]
>
> (FT 357—358)

Further Reading

The critical and scholarly literature on Proust is immense and very valuable. The following list names works that I think are of strong immediate interest and to which I owe special debts of gratitude.

Maurice Bardèche, *Marcel Proust romancier*. Paris: Les Sept Couleurs, 1971.

Samuel Beckett, *Proust*. London: John Calder, 1965.

Leo Bersani, *Marcel Proust: The Fictions of Life and Art*. Oxford: Oxford University Press, 1965.

Malcolm Bowie, *Proust among the Stars*. London: HarperCollins, 1998.

Antoine Compagnon, *Proust entre deux siècles*. Paris: Seuil, 1989.

Miguel de Beistegui, *Jouissance de Proust: Pour une esthétique de la métaphore*. Paris: Encre marine, 2007.

René de Chantal, *Marcel Proust critique littéraire*. Montreal: Presses de l'université de Montreal, 1967.

Gilles Deleuze, *Proust et les signes*. Rennes: Presses universitaires de France, 1970.

David Ellison, *The Reading of Proust*. Baltimore, MD: Johns Hopkins, 1984.

Gerard Genette, *Figures III*. Paris: Seuil, 1972.

Margaret Gray, *Postmodern Proust*. Philadelphia, PA: University of Pennsylvania Press, 1992.

Anne Henry, *Proust romancier: Le tombeau égpytien*. Paris: Flammarion, 1983.

Edward J. Hughes, *Marcel Proust: A Study in the Quality of Awareness*. Cambridge: Cambridge University Press, 1983.

Julia Kristeva, *Le temps sensible: Proust et l'expérience littéraire*. Paris: Gallimard, 1994.

Elizabeth Ladenson, *Proust's Lesbianism*. Ithaca, NY: Cornell University Press, 1999.

Joshua Landy, *Philosophy as Fiction*. Oxford: Oxford University Press, 2004.

Joshua Landy, *The World According to Proust*. Oxford: Oxford University Press, 2023.

Michael Lucey, *What Proust Heard*. Chicago, IL: University of Chicago Press, 2022.

Jean Milly, *Proust et le style*. Paris: Les Lettres Modernes, 1970.

Anka Mulhstein, *Monsieur Proust's Library*. New York: Other Press, 2012.

Jean-Jacques Nattiez, *Proust musicien*. Paris: Christian Bourgeois, 1984.

Georges Poulet, *L'espace proustien*. Paris: Gallimard, 1963.

Christopher Prendergast, *Mirages and Mad Beliefs: Proust the Skeptic*. Princeton, NJ: Princeton University Press, 2013.

Christopher Prendergast *Living and Dying with Marcel Proust*. New York: Europa, 2022.

Jean-Pierre Richard, *Proust et le monde sensible*. Paris: Seuil, 1974.

Julius E. Rivers, *Proust and the Art of Love*. New York: Columbia University Press, 1980.

Anne Simon, *Proust ou le réel retrouvé*. Rennes: Presses universitaires de France, 2000.

Jean-Yves Tadié, *Marcel Proust: Biographie*. Paris: Gallimard, 1996.

Benjamin Taylor, *Proust: the Search*. New Haven, CT: Yale University Press, 2015.

Edmund White, *Marcel Proust*. New York: Viking Penguin, 1999.

Alison Winton, *Proust's Additions*. Cambridge: Cambridge University Press, 1977.

Notes

The main points of textual reference for Proust's work are:

Jean Santeuil, précédé de *Les Plaisirs et les jours*, ed. Pierre Clarac. Paris: Gallimard, 1971.

Albertine disparue, ed. Mauriac and Etienne Wolff. Paris: Bernard Grasset, 1987.

A la recherche du temps perdu, 4 vols, ed. Jean-Yves Tadié. Paris: Gallimard, 1987–1989.

Les Soixante-quinze feuillets, ed. Nathalie Mauriac Dyer. Paris: Gallimard, 2021.

Essais, ed. Antoine Compagnon (Christophe Pradeau and Matthieu Vernet). Paris: Gallimard, 2022.

Preface

1. John Forrester, *Thinking in Cases*. New York: Polity, 2016, p. 40.
2. In his preface to Marcel Proust, *Contre Sainte-Beuve*, ed. Bernard de Fallois. Paris: Gallimard, 1954, p. 7.
3. Jean-Yves Tadié, *Marcel Proust: Biographie*. Paris: Gallimard, 1996, p. 603.
4. Benjamin Taylor, *Proust: The Search*. New Haven, CT: Yale University Press, 2015, p. 31.
5. Marcel Proust, *In Search of Lost Time*, vol 5 *The Prisoner* (tr Carol Clark) and vol 6 *The Fugitive* (tr Peter Collier). London: Penguin, p. 181
   Further quotations from Proust's works are also in English and are taken from the books listed below. Page references appear in the text with the indicated initials.
   Jean Santeuil, tr. Gerard Hopkins. London: Weidenfeld and Nicholson, 1955. Cited as JS.
   By Way of Sainte-Beuve, tr. Sylvia Townsend Warner. London: Hogarth, 1984. Cited as BW.

In Search of Lost Time, ed. Christopher Prendergast. London: Penguin, 2002. The titles of the individual volumes are:

1. *The Way by Swann's*, tr. Lydia Davis. Cited as WS.
2. *In the Shadow of Young Girls in Flower*, tr. James Grieve. Cited as SYG.
3. *The Guermantes Way*, tr. Mark Treharne. Cited as GW.
4. *Sodom and Gomorrah*, tr. John Sturrock. Cited as SG.
5. *The Prisoner*, tr. Carol Clark; *The Fugitive*, tr. Peter Collier. Cited as P and F.
6. *Finding Time Again*, tr. Ian Patterson. Cited as FT.

Pleasures and Days, tr. Andrew Brown. London: Alma, 2013. Cited as PD. The translations of passages from the following works are my own: *Albertine disparue*. Paris: Bernard Grasset, 1987. Cited as *Albertine*. *Les Soixante-quinze feuillets*. Paris: Gallimard, 2021. Cited as *Feuillets*. 'Sentiments filiaux d'un parricide', *Essais*. Paris: Gallimard, 2022. Cited as 'Sentiments'.
6. Michel Foucault, *The Order of Things: An Archeology of the Human Sciences*. New York: Vintage, 1994, p. xv.
7. Jorge Luis Borges, 'The Analytical Language of John Wilkins', in *Other Inquisitions*, tr. Ruth L. C. Simms. New York: Washington Square Press, 1966, p. 108.
8. Foucault, *The Order of Things*, pp. xvii, xxi, xxiv.
9. Franz Kafka, 'Brief an den Vater', in Max Brod, ed., *Hochzeitsvorbereitungen auf dem Lande*. Frankfurt a.M: Fischer, 1991, p. 124.

Chapter 1

1. Antoine Compagnon, 'La "Recherche du temps perdu" de Marcel Proust', in Pierre Nora, ed., *Les Lieux de mémoire*, vol. 3. Paris: Gallimard, 1997, pp. 3850, 3861.
2. Marcel Proust, *Lettres*, ed. Francois Leriche (Caroline Szylowicz). Paris: Plon, 2004, p. 608.
3. T. S. Eliot, *Selected Prose*. San Diego, CA: Harcourt Brace Jovanovich, 1975, p. 177.
4. Thomas Mann, *The Magic Mountain*, tr. John E. Woods. London: Folio Society, 1995, p. xv.

5. Compagnon, 'La "Recherche du temps perdu" de Marcel Proust', p. 3857.
6. Marcel Proust, *Contre Sainte-Beuve*, ed. Bernard de Fallois. Paris: Gallimard, 1954, p. 11.
7. I should say something about the profusion of texts called *Contre Sainte-Beuve*. There is de Fallois's selection, published in 1954. There is a more scholarly and less eclectic text edited by Pierre Clarac and Yves Sandre, published in 1971. On their first page, the editors anticipate our surprise ('on s'étonnera peut-être') at the difference between their *Contre Sainte-Beuve* and its predecessor. The material also appears in the 2022 collection of Proust's essays. The editor, Antoine Compagnon, reminds us that *Contre Sainte-Beuve*, as a book, doesn't exist; he is offering not a third version but a 'dossier' on the relevant writing.

There are two English translations: of the de Fallois text by Sylvia Townsend Warner, published in 1958; of the Clarac/Sandre text by John Sturrock, published in 1988. I have quoted from the Townsend Warner version because of the context and the relevance of de Fallois's selection.
8. Céleste Albaret, *Monsieur Proust*. Paris: Laffont, 1973, p. 346.
9. W. B. Yeats, *Essays and Introductions*. New York: Macmillan, 1961, p. 509.
10. Quoted in Christopher Prendergast, *The Classic: Sainte-Beuve and the Nineteenth-Century Culture Wars*. Oxford: Oxford University Press, 2007, p. 2.
11. Gérard de Nerval, *Oeuvres complètes*, vol. 1. Paris: Gallimard, 1989, p. 339.

Chapter 2

1. 'Journées de lecture', in Antoine Compagnon, ed., *Essais*. Paris: Gallimard, 2022, p. 172.
2. Charles Dickens, *Little Dorrit*. New York: Dover, 2018, p. 1.
3. Marcel Proust, *In Search of Lost Time: Swann's Way*. Adaptation and Drawings by Stephane Heuet. Translated by Arthur Goldhammer. New York: Liveright, 2015.
4. James Joyce, *Ulysses*. London: Penguin, 1986, p. 113.
5. Don Gifford and Robert Seidman, *Ulysses Annotated*. Oakland, CA: University of California Press, 1989, p. 146.
6. André Maurois, *A la recherche de Marcel Proust*. London: Hachette, 1985, p. 19.

7. George D. Painter, *Marcel Proust*. London: Penguin, 1983, p. 9.
8. Roger Duchêne, *L'Impossible Marcel Proust*. Paris: Laffont, 1994, p. 22.
9. Jean-Yves Tadié, *Marcel Proust: Biographie*. Paris: Gallimard, 1996, pp. 62, 64.
10. Bertolt Brecht, *Diaries 1920–1922*, tr. John Willett. New York: St Martin's Press, 1979, p. 146.
11. Walter Benjamin, 'The Image of Proust', in *Illuminations*, tr. Harry Zohn. New York: Schocken, 1969, p. 202.

Chapter 3

1. Alain Badiou, *L'être et l'événement*. Paris: Seuil, 1998, p. 199.
2. Joachim Kalka, *Gaslight: Lantern Slides from the Nineteenth Century*, tr. Isabel Fargo Cole. New York: New York Review Books, 2017, pp. 111–112.
3. Ruth Harris, *Dreyfus: Politics, Emotion and the Scandal of the Century*. New York: Henry Holt, 2010, p. 9.
4. Emile Zola, *The Dreyfus Affair*. New Haven, CT: Yale University Press, 1996, pp. 43, 45.
5. Zola, *The Dreyfus Affair*, p. 46.
6. Marcel Proust, *Lettres*. Paris: Plon, 2004, p. 165.
7. Oscar Wilde, 'The Decay of Lying', in Mark Martin, ed., *In Praise of Disobedience*. London: Verso, 2018, p. 70.
8. Jean-Denis Bredin, *The Affair: The Case of Alfred Dreyfus*, tr. Jeffrey Mehlman. London: Sidgwick & Jackson, 1987, p. 96.
9. Alfred Dreyfus, *Lettres à la Marquise*. Paris: Bernard Grasset, 2017, p. 125.
10. Géraldi Leroy, 'Les romans de l'affaire Dreyfus', in Michel Winock, ed., *L'affaire Dreyfus*. Paris: Seuil, 1998, p. 181.
11. Marcel Proust, *Jean Santeuil*, ed. Pierre Clarac and Yves Sandre. Paris: Gallimard, 1971, p. 1059.
12. Ruth Harris, *Dreyfus*, p. 168.
13. Friedrich Nietzsche, *Writings from the Late Notebooks*, tr. Kate Sturge. Cambridge: Cambridge University Press, 2003, p. 139.
14. Jacques Derrida, *De la grammatologie*. Paris: Editions de Minuit, 1967, p. 227.
15. Rainer Maria Rilke, *The Duino Elegies*, tr. Edgar Snow. Blackburn: North Point, 2001, pp. 4–5.
16. Alfred Dreyfus, *Cinq années de ma vie*. Paris: Charpentier, 1901, p. 224.

17. Philippe Oriol, *L'histoire de l'affaire Dreyfus*, vol. 1. Paris: Stock, 2008, p. 120.

18. Marcel Thomas, *L'Affaire sans Dreyfus*. Paris: Fayard, 1971, p. 70.

Chapter 4

1. Samuel Johnson, *The Lives of the Poets*. Oxford: Oxford University Press, 2009, p. 16.

2. Malcolm Bowie, *Proust among the Stars*. London: HarperCollins, 1998, p. 18.

3. Marcel Proust, *A la recherche du temps perdu*, vol IV, ed. Yves Baudelle, Anne Chevalier, Eugène Nicole, Pierre-Louis Rey, Pierre-Edmond Robert, Jacques Robichez, and Brian Rogers. Paris: Gallimard, 1989, p. 1265.; Proust, *Correspondance*, vol VII, ed. Philp Kolb. Paris: Plon, 1981, p. 167.

4. George Eliot, *The Mill on the Floss*. London: Penguin, 2003, p. 147.

5. George Eliot, *Middlemarch*. London: Penguin, 1994, p. 85.

6. Eliot, *Middlemarch*, p. 469.

7. Marcel Proust, *Essais*, ed. Antoine Compagnon (Christophe Pradeau and Matthieu Vernet). Paris: Gallimard, 2022, p. 1220.

8. Christopher Prendergast, *Mirages and Mad Beliefs*. Princeton, NJ: Princeton University Press, 2013, p. 122.

9. Marcel Proust, *Matinée chez la Princesse de Guermantes*, ed. Henri Bonnet (Bernard Brun). Paris: Gallimard, 1982, p. 160.

10. Proust, *Matinée chez la Princesse de Guermantes*, p. 213.

11. Hesiod, *Theogony*, tr. Norman O. Brown. Indianapolis, IN: Bobbs Merrill, 1953, p. 53.

Chapter 5

1. Christopher Prendergast, *Living and Dying with Marcel Proust*. New York: Europa, 2022, p. 43.

2. Barbara Cassin (ed.), *Vocabulaire européen des philosophies*. Paris: Seuil, 2004, p. xviii.

3. Marcel Proust, *A la recherche du temps perdu*, vol. IV, ed. Yves Baudelle, Anne Chevalier, Eugène Nicole, Pierre-Louis Rey, Pierre-Edmond Robert, Jacques Robichez, and Brian Rogers. Paris: Gallimard, 1989, p. 3.

4. Marcel Proust, *Remembrance of Things Past*. vol. 3, tr. C. K. Scott Moncrieff, Terence Kilmartin, Andreas Mayor. London: Penguin, 1981, p. 425.
5. Malcolm Bull, *On Mercy*. Princeton, NJ: Princeton University Press, 2019, passim.
6. Malcolm Bowie, *Proust among the Stars*. London: HarperCollins, 1998, p. 44.

Chapter 6

1. Jean-Pierre Richard, *Proust et le monde sensible*. Paris: Seuil, 1974, pp. 231–232, 233.
2. David Ellison, *A Reader's Guide to Proust's In Search of Lost Time*. Cambridge: Cambridge University Press, 2010, p. 170.
3. Marcel Proust, *Essais*, ed. Antoine Compagnon (Christophe Pradeau and Matthieu Vernet). Paris: Gallimard, 2022, p. 1287.
4. Jacqueline Rose, *Albertine*. New York: Vintage, 2002, p. 65.
5. Marcel Proust, *Lettres*. Paris: Plon, 2004, p. 364.
6. Antoine Compagnon, 'Truth and Justice', in André Benhaïm, ed., *The Strange M Proust*. London: Routledge, 2020, p. 120.
7. Compagnon, 'Truth and Justice', p. 120.
8. Fyodor Dostoevsky, *The Brothers Karamazov*, tr. Richard Pevear and Larissa Volokhonsky. New York: Farrar, Straus and Giroux, 1990, p. 509.
9. Theodor Adorno, *Minima Moralia*, tr. E. F. N. Jephcott. London: Verso, 1974, p. 163.

Chapter 7

1. Charles Dickens, *Bleak House*. London: Penguin, 2003, p. 27.
2. Charles Dickens, *David Copperfield*. London: Penguin, 2004, p. 13.
3. Antoine Compagnon, 'La "Recherche du temps perdu" de Marcel Proust', in Pierre Nora, ed., *Les Lieux de mémoire*, vol. 3. Paris: Gallimard, 1997, p. 3864.
4. Fyodor Dostoevsky, *The Adolescent*, tr. Richard Pevear and Larissa Volokhonsky. New York: Vintage, 2004, p. 10.
5. Jean Milly, notes to *La Prisonnière*. Paris: Flammarion, 1984, p. 537.
6. Milly, notes to *La Prisonnière*, p. 531.

7. Marcel Proust, *Matinée chez la Princesse de Guermantes*, ed. Henri Bonnet (Bernard Brun). Paris: Gallimard, 1982, p. 197.
8. Milly, notes to *La Prisonnière*, p. 531.
9. Franz Kafka, *Parables and Paradoxes*. New York: Schocken, 1961, pp. 80–81.
10. Céleste Albaret, *Monsieur Proust*. Paris: Laffont, 1973, p. 429.
11. Jean-Yves Tadié, *Marcel Proust: Biographie*. Paris: Gallimard, 1996, pp. 892–894.
12. Marcel Proust, *Carnets*, ed. Florence Callu and Antoine Compagnon. Paris: Gallimard, 2002, p. 89.

Index

Adorno, T. W. 105
Albaret, Céleste 5, 117
Austen, Jane 111, 114

Badiou, Alain 37–38
Balzac, Honoré de 2–4, 12–13, 38–39, 54
Barthes, Roland 11
Baudelaire, Charles 4, 11–12, 92–93
Begley, Louis 104
Benjamin, Walter 26
Binet, Alfred 9
Blanchot, Maurice 3–4
Boisdeffre, Raoul de 42
Borges, Jorge Luis x, 37–38
Bowie, Malcolm 56, 79–80
Brecht, Bertolt 33
Bredin, Jean-Denis 39–40
Bull, Malcolm 79

Cassin, Barbara 78–79
Clemenceau, Georges 38, 48–49
Collier, Peter 79
Compagnon, Antoine 1, 3–4, 103, 112

Davis, Lydia 20, 59
Derrida, Jacques 51
Descartes, René 9
Dickens, Charles 20–23, 39, 87, 109, 110–111
Diesbach, Ghislain de 32–33
Donne, John 56
Dostoevsky, Fyodor 90–91, 103, 113
Dreyfus, Alfred 38–45, 48–50, 52–54, 100, 101, 104–105
Drumont, Edouard 48
Duchêne, Roger 32–33

Eliot, George 61, 111
Eliot, T. S. 2
Ellison, David 90

Esterhazy, Ferdinand Walsin 44–45, 53–54

Fallois, Bernard de viii, 1, 4–5, 7
Flaubert, Gustave 61–62
Fleming, Ian 56
Forrester, John vii
Foucault, Michel vii, x
Fraisse, Luc 5

Gifford, Don 22–23
Goncourt, Edmond de 67–68
Goncourt, Jules de 67–68

Haas, Charles 113
Hardy, Thomas 84–85
Harris, Ruth 37–38, 48–49
Henry, Hubert-Joseph 39–40, 50
Hesiod 69–70
Heuet, Stéphane 21

James, Henry 11
Johnson, Samuel 56
Joyce, James 2, 22–23, 32–33, 76

Kafka, Franz xii, 2, 72, 116
Kalka, Joachim 37–38
Kennedy, John F 39
Kermode, Frank 116

Labori, Fernand 48–49
La Bruyère, Jean de 11
Landy, Joshua 111–112
Leroy, Géraldi 41
Levin, Harry 2

Maistre, Joseph de 103
Mann, Thomas 2–3, 55
Mantegna, Andrea 56–57
Mauriac Dyer, Nathalie 4–6, 14, 17–18

INDEX

Maurois, André 32–33
Mercier, Auguste 52–53
Milly, Jean 113–116
Musil, Robert 2

Nabokov, Vladimir 109, 111
Nerval, Gerard de 4, 14, 19
Nietzsche, Friedrich 51

Painter, George 32–33
Patterson, Ian 73
Picquart, Georges 41, 43–45, 48–49
Poe, Edgar Alan Poe 92–93
Prendergast, Christopher 63–64, 74–75
Proust, Jeanne 95–96

Rabelais, François 59
Reinach, Joseph 48–49
Ribot, Théodule 93
Richard, Jean-Pierre 89
Rilke, Rainer Maria 51–52
Rose, Jacqueline 91

Sainte-Beuve, Charles Augustin 4–11
Scott Moncrieff, C. K. 20, 59, 73, 79,
    80–81

Seidman, Robert 22–23
Sévigné, Marie de 90–91
Shakespeare, William 38–39, 99
Stifter, Adalbert 2
Strauss, Geneviève 100
Sturrock, John 9

Tadié, Jean-Yves 5–6, 32–33, 117–118
Taylor, Ben viii
Thomas, Marcel 53–54, 104–105
Tissot, James 112–113
Tolstoy, Leo 12–13
Truffaut, François 32–33

Van Blarenberghe, Henri 96–99
Veronese, Paolo 56–57

Warner, Sylvia Townsend 9
Wilde, Oscar 39, 98–99
Wittgenstein, Ludwig 13
Woolf, Virginia 2

Yeats, W. B. 11

Zola, Emile 38–40, 48–49